L

# GRAN CANARIA

*a countryside guide*
### Sixth edition

## Noel Rochford

# SUNFLOWER BOOKS

**Sixth edition** © 2011
Sunflower Books™
PO Box 36160
London SW7 3WS, UK
www.sunflowerbooks.co.uk

Sunflower Books and
'Landscapes' are
Registered Trademarks

ISBN 978-1-85691-405-5

*Cave house (Walk 17)*

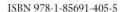

# *Important note to the reader*

We have tried to ensure that the descriptions and maps in this book are error-free at press date. The book will be updated, where necessary, whenever future printings permit. It will be very helpful for us to receive your comments (sent in care of the publishers, please) for the updating of future printings.

We also rely on those who use this book — especially walkers — to take along a good supply of common sense when they explore. Conditions change fairly rapidly in the Canary Islands, and *storm damage or bulldozing may make a route unsafe at any time*. If the route is not as we outline it here, and your way ahead is not secure, return to the point of departure. *Never attempt to complete a tour or walk under hazardous conditions!* Please read carefully the notes on pages 33-40, as well as the introductory comments at the beginning of each tour and walk (regarding road conditions, equipment, grade, distances and time, etc). Explore *safely*, while at the same time respecting the beauty of the countryside.

*Cover photograph: the sand dunes of Maspalomas*
*Title page: cave church at Artenara*

Photographs: the author, except for pages 14, 20, 26 (top right and bottom right): John Underwood; page 26 (bottom left): John Seccombe; istockphoto pages 78-79 and cover
Maps: Sunflower Books, based on the 1:50,000 maps of the Servicio Geográfico del Ejército, with permission.
Drawings: Sharon Rochford
A CIP catalogue record for this book is available from the British Library.
Printed and bound in China: WKT Company Ltd

# Contents

*View across the Vega de Acusa
(Walk 26) to Roque Bentaiga and
Roque Nublo in the far distance.*

# Preface

Every year millions of tourists flock to Gran Canaria, 'the island of eternal spring', to soak up the sun. Unfortunately, few of these sun-worshippers explore beyond the beaches.

The weather may be the island's strong point, but by no means is it Gran Canaria's *only* asset. A wealth of diverse landscapes and a wonderland of curious flora await the explorer. So special are these ecosystems, that almost half the island has been designated a nature protection or preservation area. It's hard to believe that such a small island (1532 sq km/600 sq mi) has so much to offer. And yet it has often been referred to as a 'continent in miniature'. Travel across Gran Canaria for a day — by car or on foot — and see for yourself!

The *cumbre*, the island's great saddle, is to hikers what the Playa del Inglés is to the beach freaks. From its hub ravines are born and fan out seaward like spokes on a wheel, gouging enormous valleys in their wake. For me what makes Gran Canaria so special are the magnificent *barrancos* (ravines). Each has its own little secret to share. In the Barranco de la Mina there's a cascading stream; the Barranco de la Aldea hides an emerald green *embalse* (reservoir); the Barranco de Güigüí opens out to an incomparable beach. These are but a few of the island's breathtaking ravines. Give me some time, and I'll show you a Gran Canaria not found in the glossy tourist brochures … a Gran Canaria you'll long remember.

The harsh and often inhospitable character of the countryside is softened by a wealth of flora. The slopes of the *cumbre* are like a wild garden in spring, ablaze with bright yellow *retama (Teline)* and flecked with mauve *Cheiranthus*, pale blue *Echium*, and the white to carmine florets of *Senecio*. Spacious pine woods cloak the highest summits. Palm-studded valleys and giant *Euphorbias*, like *cardón* (candelabra spurge), on the barren sea-slopes, hint of nearby Africa.

Gran Canaria has two attributes which make it quite distinct in the archipelago. The island is inundated with sites and relics of the past — the Guanche epoch. Little is known about these deeply religious and moral people. It is believed that they arrived on the islands about 4000 years ago. Vestiges of their civilisation can be found in ancient settlements, intriguing troglodyte villages carved high into often-inaccessible crags. These archaeological finds, some of them quite spectacular, bring life to your excursions. Dams and reservoirs are the second special feature of the island. These small reflections of calm water are Gran Canaria's lifeline. Every valley cradles one.

Getting out into the countryside, you leave all traces of tourism behind. Gran Canaria is not Playa del Inglés, or Puerto Rico, or Las Canteras. Hire a car or hop on a local bus, and you'll taste the real flavours of the island, as you scale the peaks, cross the *barrancos* and pass through the small and lonely hamlets. This will cost you a bit of time and energy, but you will be well rewarded.

Ramblers and ardent trekkers can chose from a large selection of graded walks. But if you're happiest with wheels under you, the car tours (and their highly-recommended detours) will keep you engrossed for days — especially if you stretch your legs to visit any of the easily-accessible picnic spots.

In the last decade the local government, with EU funding, has restored a vast network of old stone-laid trails (the *caminos reales;* see the footnote on page 34). As a result, islanders as well as tourists are now out hiking the hills. Gran Canaria is on its way to becoming a hiking mecca. *Landscapes of Gran Canaria* puts this miniature continent and its hiking trails at your fingertips.

### Acknowledgements

I'd like to express my gratitude to the following organisations and people, who helped me prepare the first few editions of this book, and with the updating of later editions: the Tourist Office and local government offices (Cabildo) in Las Palmas; Medio Ambiente; the Grupo Montañero Solidad; the Meteorological Office; the Jardín Botánico; the Patronato de Turismo; the Hotel El Refugio; Conny Spelbrink (who turns the islands inside out for me!); my publishers at Sunflower; and the Servicio Geográfico del Ejército in Madrid, for permission to adapt their large-scale maps.

### Further reading

Titles in the 'Landscapes' series are countryside guides, intended for use in tandem with a general guide — of which there are many available. Two reference books which I particularly treasure are *Wild Flowers of the Canary Islands* by David and Zoë Bramwell and *Crafts and Traditions of the Canary Islands* by Michael Eddy. Both are out of print at time of writing, but available on the web from various suppliers (at hefty prices, so try your local library first!).

If you enjoy using this book, I've written several other 'Landscapes' for the Canaries: *Tenerife (Orotava • Anaga • Teno • Cañadas); Southern Tenerife and La Gomera; La Palma and El Hierro; Lanzarote; Fuerteventura* (all published by Sunflower Books).

# ● Getting about

There is no doubt that a **hired car** is the most convenient way of getting about on Gran Canaria. And the second most flexible form of transport is of course the **taxi**. Both cars and taxis are especially economical if three or four people are sharing the cost.

**Coach tours** are the most popular way of 'seeing the island in a day'. They provide a painless introduction to road conditions and a remarkable overview of island scenery. You will discover in comfort the landscapes you will want to explore at leisure, on your own.

My favourite way of getting about is by *guagua* — **local bus** (pronounced 'gwah-gwah'). The bus network on Gran Canaria is very comprehensive, economical and fun! You get splendid views, too, perched up on bus seats, as you bump your way around the island. The plans on the fold-out touring map show you where to find your buses in Las Palmas and the Playa del Inglés/Maspalomas conurbation.

On pages 128 to 133 you will find timetables for all the buses used for the walks and picnics in this book. *Please do not rely solely on the timetables included here;* changes to schedules are fairly frequent. The bus operator is called Global, and you can download their latest timetables at www.globalsu.net. Otherwise, obtain the latest printed bus timetables from the bus station nearest your hotel. Ask, too, about discount tickets if you plan to use the buses regularly; you should be able to save at least 20-30% if you prepay a carnet with a magnetic strip *(Carné Especial EP)*, which is validated each time you use a bus (see under 'magnetic cards' on the Global website).

Since no intermediate times are shown on the Global website, *always verify* bus departures and returns for longer journeys before you set out (especially to places where the service is infrequent). It's always a good idea to *arrive a bit earlier* than the stated departure time, too ... just in case!

---

*Hint:* However you get about, *do* refer to the large-scale walking maps of the area from time to time (perhaps when you stop at a viewpoint). They contain a wealth of detail and will help you to identify many of the surrounding geographical features.

---

# ◉ Picnicking

Picnicking on Gran Canaria is tremendously enjoyable. Not only can you make your choice from many spectacular settings, but there are some lovely organised picnic sites on the island too. These have been set up by Spain's national conservation agency (Medio Ambiente) and are very well equipped with tables and benches, drinking fountains and toilets. Some have barbecue sites and play areas for children. **All roadside picnic areas with tables** (and often other facilities) are indicated both in the car touring notes and on the touring map by the symbol ⊼.

On the following pages, however, I describe my personal suggestions for picnics 'off the beaten track'. Many of them are easily accessible by bus as well as private transport and require only a short walk. All the information you need to get to these picnic spots is given on the following pages, where *picnic numbers correspond to walk numbers*, so that you can quickly find the general location on the island by looking at the pull-out touring map (where the walk locations are shown). I include transport details (🚐: access by bus; 🚗: where to park), how long a walk you'll have, and views or setting. Beside the picnic title, you'll find a map reference: the location of the picnic spot is shown on this *walking* map by the symbol *P* printed in green. Many of the picnic settings are illustrated.

Please look over the comments before you

*Charco Hondo (Picnic 12)*

start off on your picnic: if more than a few minutes' walking is required, remember to **wear stout lace-up shoes** and to **take a sunhat** (○ indicates a picnic **in full sun**). It's a good idea to take along a plastic groundsheet as well, in case the ground is damp or prickly.

**If you're travelling to your picnic by bus**, be sure to arm yourself with up-to-date bus timetables (see page 7). While there are complete timetables on pages 128-133, remember that no book can ever be as up-to-date as the timetables on the web or at the bus stations. **If you are travelling to your picnic by car**, be extra vigilant off the main roads: children and animals are often in the village streets. Without damaging plants, do park *well off* the road; *never* block a road or track.

All picnickers should read the Country code on page 39 and go quietly in the countryside.

### 1a LA CULATA OVERLOOK (map reverse of touring map)

*by car: 20-30min on foot*                    *by bus: 30-40min on foot*
🚐 18 to La Culata (Timetable 20) or 🚌: take the GC608 to La Culata, southeast of Tejeda. Pass through the village and take the first right turn, to the hamlet at the end of the road. Near Car tour 3.
*Follow Walk 1 (page 42) up to the bird's-eye viewpoint over La Culata, a climb of about 100m/330ft. Shade nearby.*

*This cross is 25min below the Mirador de los Pinos de Gáldar, but you don't have to descend very far to enjoy similar views (Picnic 5).*

## 1b PRESA DE LOS HORNOS (map on reverse of touring map, photograph page 43) ○

*by car: up to 5min on foot*      *by bus: not accessible*

🚗 Park above the reservoir, at the small *mirador* parking area on the GC600, northeast of Ayacata. Car tour 4; near Car tour 3.

*Picnic overlooking this picturesque reservoir. Popular spot, but if you follow the path that descends to cross the dam wall, you'll find peace and quiet. Limited shade nearby.*

## 3 EL TOSCON (map on reverse of touring map) ○

*by car: 5-10min on foot*      *by bus: not accessible*

🚗 Park at the side of the road, at the end of the drawn-out village of El Toscón. It's on the GC606, west of Ayacata. The turn-off is from the GC60 at the Degollada del Aserrador and is signposted 'El Juncal'. When this road forks immediately; keep right. Detour on Car tour 3.

*Just after the last house in the village you're alongside a rounded 'rock loaf'. At the top is a cross and a belfry. It's a wonderful lookout over a canyon and, in the distance, the plains of San Nicolás. No shade.*

## 4 CRUZ DE TEJEDA (map pages 52-53)

*by car: up to 10min on foot*      *by bus: up to 10 min on foot*

🚗 Car park behind the *parador* at Cruz de Tejeda. Car tour 3.

🚐 18 to Cruz de Tejeda (Timetable 20)

*Picnic anywhere on the hillside behind the* parador, *overlooking the immense Tejeda Valley. A short, steep climb of up to 80m/260ft, in the shade of pines. Note: it can be very windy here. See also Picnic 6a.*

## 5 MIRADOR DE LOS PINOS DE GALDAR (map on pages 52-53, photographs pages 56-57, 68 and above)

*by car: up to 5min on foot*      *by bus: up to 5min on foot*

🚗 Park at the *mirador* (on the GC21, 22km west of Teror and signposted). Car tour 2.

🚐 220 (Timetable 7); ask for 'Mirador de los Pinos de Gáldar'.

*Picnic in the shade of pines below the* mirador, *with views over the wooded hills of Tamadaba to Tenerife's El Teide in the distance. The descent and climb back up is steep and gravelly.*

## 6a CRUZ DE TEJEDA (map pages 52-53) ○

*by car: up to 10min on foot*      *by bus: up to 10min on foot*

🚗 and 🚐 as for Picnic 4 above.

*Use the notes on page 58 to start Walk 6 and find a quiet spot on the hillside, with superb views across the island's summits and Fuerteventura in the distance. No shade. See also Picnic 4.*

## 6b LAS CALDERETAS (map pages 52-53, photograph page 58)

*by car: 15-20min on foot*      *by bus: 15-20min on foot*

🚗 Limited parking off the GC21, south of Lanzarote, at Cuevas de

Corcho, where the road turns right for Cruz de Tejeda. Near Car tour 2.
🚌 220 (Timetable 7); alight at Cuevas de Corcho.
*Use the notes for Walk 6 from the 50min-point (page 58) to reach the overview down into the grassy crater. A traditional farmstead occupies the floor. A striking spot. Shade nearby.*

## 8 NEAR THE MIRADOR DE BECERRA (map: reverse of touring map) ○

*by car: 15-20min on foot*                              *by bus: not accessible*
🚗 Park at the Mirador de Becerra on the GC150, southeast of Cruz de Tejeda. Near Car tours 3 and 4.
*Follow Walk 8 from the 40min-point (page 66), to continue past the mirador and descend into a very picturesque side-valley tucked away in the upper Barranco de Tejeda (no shade). If you have the energy, it's worth descending an extra 15-20 minutes to the hillside streams (shade).*

## 10 BARRANCO AZUAJE (map page 72, photograph pages 70-71)

*by car: 5-10min on foot*                              *by bus: not accessible*
🚗 Park by the *barranco*. Heading west from Arucas on the GC300, turn down the very rough concrete track on the western side of the Barranco Azuaje. Park 0.3km downhill, near an enclosed spring. Car tours 1, 2.
*Cross the bridge and follow the lane off left into the ravine. Continue up the ravine as far as you like. The colonnaded-spa ruin sits unnoticed in a lush barranco dripping with verdure. A prize spot, with shade.*

## 11 BARRANCO DE GUAYADEQUE (map: reverse of touring map)

*by car: up to 5min on foot*                              *by bus: not accessible*
🚗 Park off the side of the road 0.3km beyond the picnic site at Montaña de las Tierras. The village is at the end of the GC103 out of Agüimes
(signposted for the Barranco de Guayadeque). Detour on Car tour 3. *There is an official picnic site here with tables, benches, and barbecues (but no water), in the shade of two eucalyptus trees. My favourite spot, however, is some 300m/yds further uphill along the road, on the left, below a stand of walnut trees. (This is where you should park.) From here a path climbs to a delicious, cool spring, and a strip of shady terraced hillside.*

*Tamadaba (Car tour 2; Picnic 24)*

## 12 THE CUMBRE (map on reverse of touring map, photographs pages 8-9, 80, 81) ○

*by car: 25min-1h on foot*                    *by bus: 25min-1h on foot*

🚗 Park at Cruz Grande: this is just a signposted pass on the GC60 between Ayacata and San Bartolomé. There is plenty of parking space beside the road. Car tours 3, 4.

🚌 18 (Timetable 20); ask for 'Cruz Grande'.

*Ayagaures and the Barranco de la Data (Walks 16 and 19) — this area has many attractive picnic spots, mostly in full sun.*

*Follow Walk 12 (page 77) up to the first concrete peg; a climb of 100m/ 330ft).
If you are energetic, you can continue up to the dramatically-sited Charco
Hondo, shown on pages 8-9 (a climb of 250m/ 820ft; allow 1h). Both picnic
places overlook the Ahogaderos Valley.*

## 15 BARRANCO DE LA DATA OVERLOOK (map pages 88-89) ○

*by car: 30min on foot*        *by bus: 30min on foot*
🚗 and 🚌 as for Picnic 12.
*Follow Walk 15 from Cruz Grande (the 1h20min-point, page 87) for about
30 minutes, to where the track swings sharp left. Having climbed no more than
about 60m/200ft, you enjoy good views down into the impressive canyon of the
Barranco de la Data. Limited shade nearby.*

## 17 NEAR MONTAÑA DE SANTIAGO (map pages 94-95, photograph page 2)

*by car: 20min on foot*        *by bus: 50min on foot*
🚗 Park at the Montaña de Santiago *zona recreativa* off the GC604, best
reached from the GC60 south of Ayacata. Detour on Car tours 3, 4.
🚌 18 (Timetable 20); ask for 'Montaña de Santiago'. Follow the GC604
south until you reach two tracks turning off right. Take the second one,
for 'Pinar de Santiago', to the picnic area (15 min).
*Pass through the centre of the picnic area and fork left. In 8 minutes you'll
enter a rocky valley. Follow the path descending off the track. Squeezing your
way through this small plant-congested ravine, after a few minutes you'll come
upon a deserted hamlet of cave dwellings. Shade in the barranco, one of Gran
Canaria's best-kept secrets. But note: the climb back up to the picnic area is
about 100m/328ft (20 min).*

## 18a EMBALSE DE SORIA (map pages 94-95) ○

*by car: 20-30min on foot*        *by bus: not accessible*
🚗 Park in Soria by the bar/restaurant (limited parking). Soria is north
of Arguineguín on the GC505 (the road is signposted to Cercados de
Espino). Keep left each time the road forks, but at El Baranquillo Andrés
keep *right*. Detour on Car tour 4.
*From the bar/restaurant, follow the road down to the wall of the dam. Cross it
and turn right immediately, to overlook the Barranco de Arguineguín. Or
head down to the water's edge (but don't plan to swim here; you would be too
close to the gates, should the level of the dam change quickly). No shade at either
setting.*

## 18b EMBALSE DE SORIA (map pages 94-95) ○

*by car: 5-10min on foot*        *by bus: not accessible*
🚗 Access as Picnic 18a, but park off the roadside at a fork 0.6km beyond
the bar/restaurant. Don't block the road.
*Walk down the right-hand fork signposted to Víveres Sara, then take the path
to the right of this shop/bar. At the fork a couple of minutes downhill, keep left,
to skirt a small barranco. You will come to a deserted village on a rocky outcrop
high above the dam: a picture-postcard spot, but no shade.*

## 19 ARTEARA (map pages 88-89, photograph page 32) ○

*by car: about 20-25min on foot*        *by bus: about 20-25min on foot*
🚗 Park in Arteara's car park, just off the GC60, north of Maspalomas.
Car tour 4.
🚌 18 to Arteara (Timetable 20)

*Use the notes on page 100 to start Walk 19. Explore the Guanche cemetery shown on page 32 (an easy stroll), then enjoy the view over the valley from the mirador. The nearest shade is at the stand of palms in the valley floor.*

## 24 TAMADABA FOREST (map page 121, photograph page 11) 🏕

*by car: up to 15min on foot*          *by bus: not accessible*

🚗 Park at the Medio Ambiente *zona recreativa* in the Tamadaba pine forest (on the GC216). Car tour 2.

*Use the notes on page 119 to explore this area. Wonderful picnicking on rocky ledges with striking coastal views and an outlook to El Teide on Tenerife. Some enchanting presas (small reservoirs) are about 35 minutes away — a highly recommended walk. Full facilities and shade of pines. Busy on weekends and public holidays.*

## 26 VEGA DE ACUSA (map page 121, photographs pages 4, 127) ○

*by car: 5-10min on foot*          *by bus: not accessible*

🚗 Park in the hamlet of Acusa Seca, 1.5km off the GC210, southwest of Artenara. Car tour 2.

*Use the notes for Walk 26 on page 126 to find the exquisite, unvisited cave-village shown on page 127. The only shade is from the cliff.*

# Other Medio Ambiente picnic sites

### LLANOS DE LA PEZ (see reverse of touring map) 🏕

Park at the site, on the GC600, northeast of Ayacata.
Car tour 4. Full facilities. Shade of pines.

### EMBALSE DE LA CUEVA DE LAS NIÑAS (see reverse of touring map) 🏕

Park at the site, which is on the shore of the reservoir, off the GC605.
Car tour 3. Full facilities. Shade of pines.

### PUERTO DE LA ALDEA (see touring map) 🏕

Park at the port, 4km west of San Nicolás. Car tours 1, 2. Tables and benches in the shade of trees.

*The GC607 to El Roque de Tejeda is one of the most dramatic roads on the island. The Cueva del Rey hides in the central crag; Roque Bentaiga is to the left.*

# ☀ Touring

Car hire on Gran Canaria is good value. Unless you've pre-booked a car, shop around; hire prices are competitive. In any case, check the car before you take it on the road, and make sure that the applicable motoring laws and insurance information are given to you *in writing in English*.

If you've only one day to tour the island, then I'd suggest **Tour 3**, with short side excursions to Roque Nublo and Pico de las Nieves. This suggestion, coupled with **Tour 2**, makes the ideal **two-day programme**.

The touring notes are brief: they include little history or any other information which you can obtain free from the tourist offices. Instead, I've concentrated on the 'logistics' of touring: times and distances, road conditions, and seeing parts of the island that most tourists miss. Most of all, I emphasise possibilities for **walking** and **picnicking** (the symbol *P* will alert you to a picnic spot; see pages 8-14). While some of the picnic and walk suggestions may not be suitable during a long car tour, you may see a landscape that you would like to explore at leisure another day.

**The fold-out touring map is designed to be held out opposite the touring notes** and contains all the information you will need outside the towns. The tours are all based on the capital and cultural centre, Las Palmas, and are quite easily reached from the many *casas rurales* in the north. But if you are staying in the south, note that Tours 1 and 4 run via Maspalomas, Tour 3 can be fairly quickly joined at the Embalse Cueva de las Niñas (via Mogán), but you should allow extra time for Tour 2 (best joined by first taking the motorway to Las Palmas). Plans of Las Palmas and Playa del Inglés/Maspalomas are on the touring map.

**Allow plenty of time for visits**; the times given for the tours include only brief stops at viewpoints labelled (☞) in the notes. **Never leave valuables** in the car; take them with you (theft from cars is rife). Since there are places to stay, restaurants, petrol stations, clinics and public toilets in most villages, we have only indicated them in the notes and on the map in places where you might *not* expect to find them. **Distances** quoted are *cumulative kilometres* from Las Palmas. A key to the symbols is on the touring map. **All motorists should read the Country code on page 39 and go quietly in the countryside.**

# Car tour 1: ALL ROUND THE ISLAND

## Las Palmas • Maspalomas • Mogán • San Nicolás • Puerto de las Nieves • Agaete • Gáldar • Las Palmas

*205.5km/128mi; about 7h; Exit A from Las Palmas*

En route: ⊓ at Puerto de la Aldea; Picnic (see pages 8-14) 10, (16); Walks 10, 20-22

*All roads are in good condition. The tour follows two stretches of motorway. Some motorists may find the winding roads between Maspalomas and Agaete unnerving. No petrol stations between San Nicolás and Agaete (36km). Note that the northern coastal stretch beyond San Nicolás is not recommended during or after heavy rain or strong winds, due to the possibility of rockfall: this road runs along sheer face of the escarpment, but is well built up at the sides.*

T his excursion is popular with the islanders themselves. On Sundays and holidays, these normally quiet roads really come alive! While the tour encircles the island, the route is not always along the coastline. Midway, you leave the tranquillity of an aquamarine sea and head into the desolate interior, becoming immersed in a landscape of soaring bluffs and sharp-featured valleys. Then you return to the coast, where the sweeping basin of San Nicolás paints a wide green brush-stroke onto the canvas. From here, the dramatic coastal road hangs on to the sheer mountainsides. Finally, you travel through the island's banana belt. Never far from the sea, you cross an elevated plain dissected by deep ravines.

Heading south on the Avenida Marítima del Norte, leave Las Palmas by Exit A and take the motorway (GC1) direct to the south. There's little to say about the east side of Gran Canaria — it's barren, flat and well-settled. But the mountainous interior will hold your attention. Clouds often hang over these hills like roughly-tossed sheets.

Pass the exits for San Augustín and Playa del Inglés. These resorts, at the start of one of the longest built-up strips of coast in Spain, have everything a tourist could ask ... except peace and beauty. So I suggest you make straight for the sand dunes of Maspalomas: take the Exit 47 off the motorway and follow signs for Maspalomas. At the first roundabout keep right, at the second go straight ahead; then follow signs for 'Playa' and/or 'Faro de Maspalomas'.

**El Faro** and the **sand dunes of Maspalomas ★** (60km) create a scenic strip of coastline, now encircled by the resorts of Playa del Inglés and Maspalomas. The migrating birds attracted to the lagoon that once existed here have long since disappeared, and luxury accommodation and a golf course have been built in the lovely oasis. The dunes, best seen at sunset, provide an 'Arabian Nights' backdrop to the superb but crowded beaches.

16

Returning from the lighthouse, go straight over the first roundabout and turn left at the next one, following signs for Puerto Rico (GC500). At the next roundabout follow the *white* signs for Mogán. Small bays begin to appear. Pass through **Arguineguín** (72km), then **Patalavaca** (74km). The bare coastal plain climbs into rolling ridges. **Puerto Rico** (83km), another sprawling tourist enclave, appears unexpectedly, built across a deep coastal ravine. A walkway built into the sea cliffs connects Puerto Rico and the man-made Playa de los Amadores. While the striking stretch of coastline between Puerto Rico and Puerto de Mogán has finally fallen prey to the developers, the rustic seaside village of **La Playa de Tauro** (✕△) remains unspoilt.

Soon the Barranco de Mogán interrupts the countryside, the valley floor cleared for new construction. At the junction (90km 🚏) turn left for **Puerto de Mogán★** (91.5km) — an ideal coffee-break stop. This small port with a marina still retains its fishing village charm; it is the most pleasant of the seaside resort developments. From the port continue north on the GC200. The stark countryside is now softened by the greenery of agriculture. Walk 20 ends in the hamlet of **Las Casillas** (105.5km). **Mogán** (107km) sits back deep in the valley — a cool verdant village, hemmed in by high rocky ridges.

Keeping to the main road, ignore the turn-off right for the reservoirs of Mulato and Cueva de las Niñas (visited on Car tour 3). Soon you pass an exquisite patch of colouring in the escarpment. Pull over at the *mirador* **Fuente de los Azulejos★** (109.5km 📷), to admire this spectacular array of colours — horizontal stripes of green, cream, orange and maroon. These eye-catching tuffs remind you of the island's volcanic origins.

Continue uphill. You wind over crests and around the base of the towering tableland of rock. Walk 21 circles this plateau, starting from the *mirador* at the **Degollada de la Aldea** (116km 📷). A vast upheaval of sharp, mountainous terrain rises on the left. Beyond it lies the island's most dramatically-sited beach, the Playa de Güigüí. (If you're fit, then put aside a day for the truly spectacular hike to this beach, only accessible on foot or by sea: see Shorter walk 22 and photographs pages 110-112.)

Not far above San Nicolás, you pass a turn-off left (120.5km) to the cactus park, Cactualdea. From **San Nicolás** (124.5km 🏕) use the notes for Car tour 2 (page 21) to continue back to **Las Palmas** (205.5km).

# Car tour 2: DRAMATIC NORTHWESTERN LANDSCAPES

Las Palmas • Teror • Artenara • Tamadaba • Barranco de la Aldea • San Nicolás • Puerto de las Nieves • Agaete • Gáldar • Cenobio de Valerón • Barranco Azuaje • Arucas • Las Palmas

*210km/130mi; about 8h; Exit C from Las Palmas*

En route: ⛟ at Tamadaba, Puerto de la Aldea; Picnics (see pages 8-14): 5, (6b), 10, 24, 26; Walks 4, 5, 6, 9, 10, 24, 25, 26

*Most of this tour is on narrow winding roads, some of them rough: driving will be slow. The route along the northwest coast is very high (1000m/3300ft) and precipitous, but well built up at the sides. This stretch is not recommended during or after heavy rain or strong winds, due to the danger of rockfall. (This also applies to the road through the Barranco de la Aldea.) Some motorists may find the road between Tamadaba and San Nicolás unnerving. No petrol stations between Teror and San Nicolás (73km) or San Nicolás and Agaete (36km). Low cloud and mists are not infrequent above Teror.*

**Opening hours/market days**
**Teror:** Sunday market from 09.00-16.00 in the church square; **Casa de los Patrones:** Mon-Thu, Sat from 11.00-18.00; Sun from 10.00-14.00
**Reptilandia:** daily (except 25/12 and 1/1) from 11.00-17.30
**Cenobio de Valerón:** 10.00-17.00; closed Mondays and Tuesdays

Skirting the island's central massif (the *cumbre*), you discover Gran Canaria's bucolic charms: pine and chestnut woods loosely cloaking the heights, pastureland where shepherds *do* still roam with flocks, and valleys revealing entire villages hewn out of the hillside. Deep in the interior, a sheer passageway of jagged rock leads you out to the west. Returning to the north, your route is carved high up in the escarpment walls sliding off into the sea.

Leave Las Palmas via Exit C. You're making for Teror, but at this stage you follow motorways: first the GC2 ('Agaete'), then the GC23 ('Escaleritas, Tamaraceite') and finally the CG3 ('Tamaraceite, Teror'). Then leave the motorway and take the GC21 to Teror, winding up the Barranco de Teror under the shade of enormous eucalyptus trees. The countryside is a tapestry of tarnished greens: the rocky hillsides covered in hardy xerophytic scrub and flecked with grey-green aloes. Nearing Teror, you pass the small village of **Miraflor** (✗), known for its cheese.

**Teror★** (25km ⛟MWC) lies high in the *barranco*. Wander through the streets here, to admire the traditional houses with exquisitely-carved balconies. Teror is the home of the island's patron saint, Nuestra Señora del Pino (Our Lady of the Pine). Her magnificently-attired likeness stands in the 18th-century church of the same name, in a splendid silver shrine. Other buildings of interest include the bishop's palace, the town hall, the Cistercian and Dominican convents, and the Casa de los Patrones (a 17th-century Spanish nobleman's house, now a museum of domestic furnishings). Just 2km outside the town, on the Arucas road, lies the Finca de Osorio, a well-preserved country estate with fine grounds. Walks 6 and 9 end in Teror.

Follow the signs for Valleseco and Artenara to leave the town (still GC21). The winding road climbs steadily. Ignore the GC30 right to Firgas; continue straight ahead towards Artenara on the GC21, quickly coming to the **Balcón de Zamora★** (32.5km 📷✕). In spring the hillsides are vividly splashed in yellow and purple. You look straight back down the Barranco de Teror to Las Palmas. From the *mirador* follow signposting for Artenara, quickly passing through the hillside villages of **Valleseco** (33.5km ✕🚻WC) and **Lanzarote** (34.5km ✕; *P*6b nearby), resting in a fertile pocket crammed with trees and gardens.

Climbing higher still, you pass grazing lands and magnificent bosquets of chestnut. Poplars line the road. Amidst this invigorating alpine atmosphere you reach the **Mirador de los Pinos de Gáldar** (45km 📷*P*5; Walks 5 and 9), a superb spot from which to survey the pastoral hillsides shown on pages 56-57 and 68. Below the *mirador* is the **Caldera de los Pinos de Gáldar★**, a small but deep crater. Behind you, dark gravelly slopes climb the *cumbre*.

Continue along the GC21 towards Artenara. White-faced cave dwellings peep out of the gentle, stepped valleys below you. **Artenara★** (52km ⛽🏠✕△📷WC), the island's highest village (1230m/4034ft), snuggles into the now-declining *cumbre,* overlooking the vast Tejeda Valley. Restaurante La Silla, tunnelled into the ridge, is just the place from which to absorb this grand panorama (but the restaurant itself was closed at press date). And don't miss the Santuario de la Virgen de la Cuevita, a tiny chapel carved into the rock (photograph page 1). To get there, climb the road diagonally across from the front of the church. Walk 4 ends at Artenara, and Walks 24, 25, and 26 begin here.

Leaving Artenara, descend past the park; then, at the roundabout, take the GC210 towards San Nicolás. Some 3km further on, at a junction, ignore the GC210 for San Nicolás; go straight ahead on the GC216 for Tamadaba, the pine-robed mountain ahead. You pass an unsignposted *mirador* at the **Degollada del Sargento** (57.5km 📷): Walk 23 sets out from here. The Tirma forestry house lies on your left a couple of kilometres further along. Halfway round the one-way system circling **Tamadaba**, turn right into the *zona recreativa* and camping grounds (63km ⛺△🏠WC; *P*24; photograph page 11). There are good views from the cliff tops near the camping area, but see Walk 24 (page 118) and the large-scale map on page 121 to make the most of your visit to this lovely woodland.

Leave the one-way road at Tamadaba and turn right at the first junction you encounter, to descend the GC210

*The green mirror of the Embalse del Parralillo*

towards Acusa and San Nicolás. Here you look straight down onto an elevated volcanic lava run, now a tableland of cultivation. Less than 3km downhill, you pass an easily-overlooked turn-off to the left (signposted for Acusa Seca). It leads downhill for 1.5km, to the sanctuary-like hamlet shown on page 127 (**P**26, Walk 26) — an intriguing sight.

Passing the church and the few houses of **Acusa** (76km), you descend from the tableland. The landscape becomes increasingly dramatic. Volcanic hues saturate the valley walls; the landscape is a mass of sharp lines. In spring the hillsides are flecked with white almond blossoms. As you approach the bed of the **Barranco de la Aldea**, the brilliant emerald-green **Embalse del Parralillo** suddenly appears, stretching along the valley floor. This is one of the most memorable sights of an already-breathtaking drive. Pull up at the old windmill (⏸) to marvel at your surroundings in this severe but striking gorge.

The road twists through the depths of a jagged corridor of bare rock. **San Nicolás** (98km ✝) spans the mouth of this deep *barranco*. The village is an important agricultural centre, and a mass of greenhouses occupies the entire basin, which shelters in a horseshoe of swept-back hills. From San Nicolás turn right on the GC200. Go through **Albercón**, where Walk 22 begins, and after 4km, come to **Puerto de la Aldea** (also called **Puerto de San Nicolás**; 102km ✕🍴), an especially scenic little port where the Aldea *barranco* empties out into the sea. Sheer cliffs rise up on both sides of the stony beach.

Your route along the spectacular, awe-inspiring west coast begins at the **Mirador del Balcón** (107km ⏸). From this 'balcony', you have exhilarating views along the coastal bluffs, where the island tumbles off into the sea. Hold on to your hat, if you're wearing one — the wind really howls across these cliffs! The windswept inclines nurture the *Euphorbias: tabaiba*, the bright green-leafed shrub, and *cardón* (candelabra spurge). Along the cliffs of **Andén Verde**★ (⏸ signposted, not far past the *mirador*), you'll see the bright yellow flowers of a rarer plant hanging from the cliffs: the endemic *Lotus callis-viridis*.

At the end of the descent, turn left into **Puerto de las Nieves**★ (131.5km ✝▲✕⊕), known for its excellent sea-food restaurants and fine view along the coast. The Dedo de Dios (God's Finger), a rock pinnacle, once burst up out of the sea here — an island landmark which disappeared during tropical storm Delta in 2005. If driving has made you drousy, a dip at the pleasant beach here will revive you.

**Agaete** (133.5km ⭥) is a colourful old town with narrow winding streets. Its festival time is August 4th to 7th, when the 'Bajada de la Rama' (Lowering of the Branch) is celebrated here and at Puerto de las Nieves. Branches of pine from the Tamadaba Forest are lowered into the sea to invoke adequate rainfall during the coming months — crucial for this important agricultural centre. *Detour:* If you have time, I highly recommend a 14km return detour from here through the Agaete Valley to the once-popular spa of Los Berrazales (⛰⛏); this exuberant and productive valley is the setting for Walks 24 and 25.

The main tour continues along the GC2, through a stark landscape. *Detour:* Some 5km beyond Agaete, you could take the turn-off for Hoyo de la Piñeda and, at the roundabout, follow signs to Reptilandia★. This small zoo boasts a magnificent collection of reptiles; it is one of only four zoos in Europe where you can see the Komodo dragon — the world's largest lizard.

**Gáldar★** (142.5km ⭥△M), the ancient stronghold of the Guanches, huddles around the base of the Pico de Gáldar, a perfectly-shaped volcanic cone. The font in front of the 18th-century church of Santiago de los Caballeros here is said to have been used to baptise Guanches converted to Christianity. The church itself contains artefacts dating back to the 16th century, and there are a few modest Guanche relics in the town hall, where the courtyard boasts the island's oldest dragon tree.

Leave the GC2 following signs for Guía and continue east on the GC292. Squeeze through **Guía** (⭥), a village known for its cheese, and from there follow signposting for Cenobio de Valerón, ignoring the turn-off right to Artenara (GC70). You pass a roadside *mirador* (149.5km 📷) with an impressive view down into a deep ravine and out along the coast as far as Las Palmas. **Cenobio de Valerón★** (150km ∩📷) consists of masses of small caves sheltering under a lip of lava. Legend has it that the virgin daughters of nobility were sequestered here before marriage and fed a special diet to make them plump and attractive! The more practical explanation however, is that they were granaries.

Now head back the way you came towards Guía, but take the turn-off left for Artenara (GC70). After 5km turn left again for Moya (GC700). Climbing through tricklings of settlement and along the farmed hillsides, you reach the upper confines of the Barranco de Moya. The village of Moya sits precariously on the far wall of the *barranco*. The depths of this enormous plunging ravine harbour the remains of a great laurel forest dating back to the Tertiary period. In the ravine floor turn right (166km) on a narrow road signposted 'Barranco del Laurel' which winds up through this forest, **Los Tilos** (or **Los Tiles**)★. The forest itself (where walking is prohibited) ends less than 1.5km uphill, but the rally drivers among you may wish to venture a further 1.5km up this spectacular ravine to a turning circle from where you can safely head back. *(Note that this further stretch is not recommended for inexperienced drivers, as it's a single-lane road and vertiginous in stretches.)* Several farm plots are ensconced this jungle-like *barranco*.

As you come into **Moya** (171.5km ♣M), keep straight ahead, to visit the village's prominent twin-towered church. It occupies the same precarious site as all its predecessors, which date from the early 1500s. If you're feeling peckish, park by the fountain and try Bar Los Tilos for some good wholesome (and reasonably-priced) snacks. Leaving the village, turn right below the fountain and follow the signs for Las Palmas, to continue along the winding GC75. Turning right on the GC350 for Arucas, you descend into yet another breathtaking ravine — the **Barranco Azuaje**. Just before crossing the *barranco*, turn off right (176.5km) down a rough lane to the ravine floor. Some 0.3km along, you're greeted by the most unexpected sight: the ruins of the grand old spa shown on pages 70-71 (**P**10). Park in the parking area just below it and use the notes for Walk 10 to explore this little-known, lush spot.

Then continue along the GC300 to the pleasant country town of **Arucas** (184km ♣M※), hidden amidst vast banana plantations. You might like to visit the botanical garden here, with its excellent collection of exotic island flora. As you follow the one way-system through the town, watch for tiny signs to 'Montaña de Arucas'. These direct you up through the back streets of the old quarter, in the shadow of the imposing neo-Gothic cathedral. The finale of your tour is the panoramic view from the top of **Montaña de Arucas** (190.5km ※⌾), from where you look out over the surrounding hills back up to the *cumbre*.

Back on the main street below the cathedral, turn left and, 500m further on, turn right for 'Las Palmas' (GC20), passing below the GC300. Keep straight across a round-about, descend to the GC2 motorway, and turn right for **Las Palmas** (210km).

# Car tour 3: THE 'CONTINENT IN MINIATURE'

Las Palmas • Tafira • San Mateo • Cruz de Tejeda •
Tejeda • Cueva del Rey • Embalse de la Cueva de las
Niñas • San Bartolomé • Santa Lucía • Agüimes • Las
Palmas

*170km/105mi; about 6h (but allow plenty of extra time for each detour you make); Exit B from Las Palmas*

En route: ⊓ at the Embalse de la Cueva de las Niñas, (Montaña de las Tierras); Picnics (see pages 8-14): (1a), (3), 4, 6a, (8, 11), 12, 15, (17); Walks: (1), 2, (3), 4-8, (11), 12, 13, 15-17, (18)

*Variable, but generally good roads. The route across the* cumbre *(the central massif) is winding, narrow and sometimes shrouded in mist. Motorway traffic is likely to be very heavy on the return to Las Palmas. There are no petrol stations between Tejeda and San Bartolomé (51km).*

**Opening hours/market days**
**Jardín Canario (Tafira Alta):** open 08.00-12.00 and 13.00-18.00 (Mon-Sat), 11.00-17.00 (Sun/holidays)
**San Mateo:** Saturday afternoon/Sunday morning market
**La Cantonera (San Mateo):** museum open Mon-Fri from 10.00-13.00
**Bentaiga Archaeological Park Interpretation Centre**: open Tue-Sun from 10.00-16.00

N ow you'll see why Gran Canaria has been called 'a continent in miniature'. Over every crest lies something new. You set out in a lush landscape that rolls off the back of the northern escarpment, to climb the *cumbre*. Once over the main divide, the emerald hues give way to more subtle shades of green, as rocky abutments rupture the terrain. Palm-adorned villages, and picture-postcard reservoirs soften the harsh and rugged interior.

Head south on the Avenida Marítima del Norte and take the well-signposted Tafira turn-off (Exit B). Not far past the turn-off to the splendid **Jardín Canario** (❀) the motorway divides; keep right for **Tafira Alta** (13km) — beyond which the motorway becomes a narrow two-laned road (GC15). **Monte Lentiscal** (15km) and **Santa Brígida** (19km) are residential areas — enclaves for the wealthy and expatriates. Exotic plants and colourful gardens flank the route; eucalyptus trees line the roadside, and palms ornament the landscape.

By the time you reach **San Mateo** (26km **M**), you're well into the countryside. This productive little farming town, where Walk 12 ends, spreads across a hilly basin overflowing with garden plots and orchards. Its Saturday afternoon/Sunday morning market is lively and crowded with *local* people. La Cantonera, an ethnological museum, is also a small hotel and restaurant (open daily for lunch and Saturday evenings only for dinner). Remain on the GC15, passing through the village. Just beyond the turn-

24

off to Las Lagunetas (34.5km), you cross the Barranco de la Mina. This narrow ravine harbours a wild garden of flora and a tumbling stream. Walk 7 would take you all the way up this little-visited valley.

The tortuous 1500m/5000ft ascent ends on the roof of the island, at **Cruz de Tejeda★** (40km ▲×☜*P*4, 6a, (8)), setting for Walks 4-8. There is a lovely government *parador* here. The rugged interior stretches out before you, with razor-sharp ridges ploughing up the landscape. Roque Nublo, the monolith to the left, and Roque Bentaiga, just opposite, are the two most impressive landmarks. Below you, the Barranco de Tejeda (Walk 2) twists its way westwards, in an attempt to slice the island in two.

Still the road winds, now descending. Villages no longer sprawl across the slopes. The interior is desolate, the villages isolated. *Detour:* If you've started out early, you might like to make an 8km return detour now to La Culata, at the very end of the Tejeda Valley (*P*1a; photograph page 60). If so, turn left on the GC156 or GC608. Walk 1 begins in this village.

The main tour continues straight on to **Tejeda** (49km ♦☜). Walk 2 sets out from this attractive rural settlement, shown overleaf. Take a break here, and try some of the local sugar-laden marzipan cake and biscuits.

Leave Tejeda on the GC60 (signposted to San Bartolomé), then take the first right turn, the GC607. For the moment, ignore the road (GC671) to Roque Bentaiga. Continue on the GC607 towards El Chorillo, in the dramatic setting shown on page 14 (this narrow road may prove unnerving for inexperienced motorists). Where the road bends right to La Higuerilla, continue straight on to the hamlet of **El Roque de Tejeda** (the first group of houses set in the ridge above the road; 57km). This is the site of an ancient Guanche stronghold. The huge **Cueva del Rey★** (King's Cave), the showpiece of this great perforated crag, is *not* signposted, so few tourists see it.*

---

*Adventurous, sure-footed walkers might like to park here and visit this cave. To get there, walk up the lane into El Roque. Then climb the concrete ramp on the left. (A steep ascent follows, very close to the edge of the escarpment, and some walkers will find short stretches unnerving). Zigzag up above the garage of the first house, in a couple of minutes heading left, climbing above a TV aerial. Caves begin appearing. After five minutes uphill you will be facing the northwest, towards the Barranco de Tejeda. When you spot three almond trees below you, climb the steps above them, to the Cueva del Rey, the seat of the once-great Guanche kingdom. From the outside, the cave is nothing special. Inside, however, it measures some 70 square metres!

*Top: canal followed in Walk 2 in the Tejeda Valley (left); caves at El Roque de Tejeda, near the Cueva del Rey (middle); the GC607 near El Roque de Tejeda (right; see also photograph page 14). Bottom: La Cantonera in San Mateo (left) and the church at Tejeda (right).*

Returning from El Roque, take the first right turn to **Roque Bentaiga★**, and drive up to the modest but interesting **Bentaiga Archeological Park Interpretation Centre** (61.5km **M** 📷 and bar). If you are sure-footed and have a head for heights, you can climb an easily-seen path from here to a Guanche sanctuary — an altar carved into a crest. Although there's little to see, the perch itself is well worth the 20-minute climb.

Back on the GC60, continue south. The rocky slopes become bolder as they bulge out of the landscape. Almond trees are the sole survivors in this rugged terrain. *Detour:* Early birds may like to make a 20km return detour to El Carrizal — my favourite village, with my favourite bar. To get there, turn off right at 68.5km for 'El Juncal'. At the fork encountered immediately, keep right on the GC606. You will pass El Toscón 📷*P3*) after 5km and, after 10km, come to El Carrizal (✕📷), the tiny gem of a hamlet shown on page 48 and the cover. Lost to the world amidst formidable gulches, this is one of the settings for Walk 3.

The main tour passes the El Juncal turn-off and takes the *next* right turn, just before Ayacata — the GC605 signposted for 'Presa Las Niñas'. Short walk 18 begins some 9km downhill, at the first turn-off left (for Soria). Don't miss it! Just 1.2km further on you reach the scenically-located **Embalse de la Cueva de las Niñas** (79km △🛏 with barbecues; WC). This reservoir rests in an elevated bumpy basin on the edge of the Ojeda, Inagua and Pajonales Nature Reserve. Note: the track down to the picnic area is very rough!

From here the main tour heads back up the GC605 to Ayacata. *Detour:* A spectacular 13km return detour along the GC605 down towards Mogán through the upper reaches of the precipitous Barranco de Mogán is a must for those with the time. Keep ahead on the GC605, past the turn-off to Soria, until you reach the GC200 to Mogán, then turn back and continue up to Ayacata. If you're tempted to add on the out-and-back stretch to Soria and its impressive dam, allow another 9km return and see notes on page 32.

**Ayacata** (89km), where Alternative walk 1 ends, sits in the shadows of high rocky abutments. From here follow the GC60 towards San Bartolomé. *Detour:* A little over 3km along, you could make a sortie to a delightful tiny ravine crammed with an assortment of vegetation and a number of curious little cave dwellings. To reach it, turn right for the 'Embalse de Chira' on the GC604. Then, 0.9km along, turn right and then immediately left, for the Montaña de Santiago picnic area (*P*17). Use the notes for Picnic 17 on page 13 to reach the ravine.

The main tour continues to **Cruz Grande** (*P*12, 15), a signposted pass. Walks 12 and 17 begin here, and it's a staging-post on Walk 15. Here you begin your descent into the enormous Barranco de Tirajana. The prominent white and pink fractured rock protruding from the wall of the *cumbre* (Risco Blanco) is this valley's landmark. An extended circle of mountains encloses this basin.

**San Bartolomé** (100km 🖼), where Walks 15 and 16 begin, is a quiet agricultural town set on a hillside shelf high above the Barranco de Tirajana. At the junction just outside the town, bear left for Santa Lucía on the GC65. A winding road takes you down into the Barranco de Tirajana. Beyond **Rosiana** (🍴), you climb to the picturesque village of **Santa Lucía** (107km M 🖼). The *cumbre* rises abruptly up behind it, and palms litter the surrounding slopes. Walk 13 ends here. Grab a loaf of the village's superb bread to take home. On the outskirts of Santa Lucía take the first turn-off right, remaining on the GC65. Descending once again into the immense Tirajana Valley, discreet hamlets shelter amongst pockets of palms.

Just over 2km along, turn off right (on the GC651) for 'La Sorrueda', and turn right again to the **Mirador de La Sorrueda** (110.5km ☎). Unlike most *miradors*, you go *down* to this one — gaining a fine impression of being right inside the Caldera de Tirajana. A small but majestic reservoir, the Embalse de Tirajana, lies in the *caldera* directly below. A rock island rises up from its tail end, and palm groves decorate the valley walls. Returning from the *mirador*, turn right to a fortress-like rock, the **Fortaleza de Ansite★** (111.5km), site of the Guanches' final resistance against their Spanish conquerors. In 2010 a museum and interpretation centre will open here. A short circuit on foot leads through a natural 40km-long tunnel and back along the rocky ridge, surrounded by wonderful scenery.

Now head back to the turn-off just outside Santa Lucía, and turn sharp right on the GC550 for Temisas and Ingenio. This stretch of road may be unnerving for some motorists, but there are guard rails. Wind your way across desolate countryside, the only greenery emanating from the xerophytic vegetation. You pass through **Temisas**, a pretty village set amidst olive groves, and then descend towards Agüimes. Turn left at a T-junction and, in the centre of **Agüimes** (133km ♣) ignore the fork to the right.

*Detour:* If you're not all 'detoured-out', a 16km return drive up the impressive Barranco de Guayadeque★ (where there is an excellent information centre; see footnote on page 73) will round your day off nicely. The turn-off to this *barranco* is a narrow *(easily missed)* street forking left 0.5km beyond the junction in the centre of Agüimes. There's a tiny signpost opposite the turn-off. This *barranco* is known for its ancient Guanche cave dwellings (although they are not easily accessible). Deep in the valley are two curious hamlets, both carved into the sheer *barranco* walls: Guayadeque (♣✕) and Montaña de las Tierras (✕📷⅋ *P*11), where Walk 11 starts. Visit the bars and restaurants in these hamlets; they too have been carved out of rock. If you're a walker, you might save this visit for another day, when you could combine the drive with a short walk.

From Agüimes the main tour follows the GC100 towards Telde. At **Ingenio** head straight down the GC196 to the GC1 motorway and turn left, back to **Las Palmas** (170km).

# Car tour 4: ACROSS THE *CUMBRE*

## Las Palmas • Monte Lentiscal • Caldera de Bandama • Telde • Pico de las Nieves • Ayacata • San Bartolomé • Fataga • Arteara • Maspalomas • Las Palmas

*166km/103mi; about 6h; Exit B from Las Palmas*

En route: 🛆 at Llanos de la Pez, (Montaña de Santiago); Picnics (see pages 8-14): 1b, 12, 15, (16, 17, 18a, 18b), 19; Walks: 1, 11-17, (18)

*The roads are in good condition generally, but are narrow. The ascent of the cumbre (central massif) is steep and winding; be prepared for mists here, too. The road from Fataga to Maspalomas is narrow and may prove unnerving for some motorists, although there are guard rails. The detour route up the Barranco de Arguineguín follows a wide road, but some stretches lack guard rails. No petrol stations between Telde and San Bartolomé (53km).*

**Opening hours**
**Museo León y Castillo, Telde:** 09.00-21.00 Mon-Fri; 10.00-13.00 Sat
**Guayere Cave Museum, La Cumbre:** 10.00-17.00 Mon-Sat
**Mundo Aborigen, Fataga:** 09.00-18.00 daily

Unlike the other tours, this excursion does not require an early morning start, unless you plan to include the detour to the Barranco de Arguineguín. Spiced with interest both geological and historical, this route offers what you might call 'value for petrol'. Crossing the *cumbre*, you'll be overwhelmed by the lushness of the island, as you crawl over the highest summits, through pine woods separated by grassy slopes. Sweeping views greet you and trail behind you. Deep in the interior, valleys of almond groves or palms lie in wait.

Set out as for Car tour 3 (page 24). At **Monte Lentiscal** (15km), turn left for Bandama on the GC802. Follow signposting to the summit, continuing up the dark, dull volcanic cone. Views unfold — first over the exclusive residential areas of Monte Lentiscal and Tafira, then onto Las Palmas and the long curving bay of Las Canteras. Vineyards nest in the coal-coloured *lapilli* hollows in the surrounding slopes. Inland, hills climb upon hills, with deep narrow gullies eating back into them. The **Caldera de Bandama★** (📷) is an impressive crater, 200m/650ft deep and more than 1km across. Use the notes and map on pages 84-86 (Walk 14) to explore the area, perhaps taking a short walk.

Back at the first junction, turn left towards La Atalaya. Coming to a junction just before that village (24km), turn left for Telde on the GC80. The lush landscape of the north has vanished. Trees no longer abound, and rocky ravines crack open the countryside. Eucalyptus, cypresses and *pinos gallegos* line the road; scatterings of hardy olives dot the slopes.

When you come to a T-junction (32km), turn left and, at the next junction (3km further on), go right, into **Telde** (35km ✝M), Gran Canaria's second-largest city. Telde, like Gáldar (Car tour 2), was once a Guanche capital. You enter the city on the GC100, and it is easiest to *stay on this ring road,* * circling the centre clockwise for just over 3km, watching carefully for your turn off (the GC130, signposted to Tejeda).

Now your ascent of the *cumbre* begins. Almost at once, you leave all settlement behind, as you twist up through hillsides covered in fine gravel. Tones of nutmeg and rust-brown, grey, and cream emanate from the roadside embankments. As you gain height, extensive views unravel below. The east is a landscape of bare volcanic knolls; the north, lighter and brighter, a turbulent sea of viridescent ridges. The Barranco de los Cernícalos falls away to your right. Almond trees cling to the herbaceous slopes. In spring the countryside is carpeted in bright yellow *retama* (photograph pages 74-75, a breathtaking sight. The **Caldera de los Marteles★** (56km 📷) takes you by surprise, 19km uphill from Telde. Bright green squares of barley patch the crater floor (photograph page 76). Loose strands of pines creep down the crests. This is cloud territory, at 1500m/5000ft, and you can be engulfed in seconds! Then, just as quickly, the views will open up again. Walk 11 crosses the cumbre here. Less than 3km further uphill you pass a track forking off left — the starting point for Walk 13.

At the **Los Pechos** junction (61km) turn left for 'Pozo las Nieves' (GC134). One kilometre further uphill, turn right (at another 'Pozo' signpost) to **Pico de las Nieves★** (📷), the island's highest point (1949m/6392ft). Walk 12 comes in here, from the nearby summit of Alto del Campanario, and the photograph on pages 78-79 shows the stupendous views across the interior that you enjoy from these peaks. The Tejeda ravine cuts across the land-scape like a gaping wound, its walls crowned by the prominent Roque Nublo (on the left) and Roque Bentaiga (straight ahead). In the distance El Teide on Tenerife rises above a cloud necklace. Return to the last junction. On the

---

*Driving through and parking in the centre of Telde is a nightmare; it is best to come by bus to take in the 15th-century church of San Juan Bautista and the nearby León y Castillo house (M), both enriched by the wealth of the *Conquistadores*. On the northern side of this urban sprawl, you'll find the older and far more attractive quarter of San Francisco, with its simple monastery church.

right is the **Pozo de las Nieves**, a deep snow pit used from about 1700 until early in the 20th century. Turn right here for 'Pico de la Gorra' (GC135); after 1km you come to another thrilling viewpoint on the right — this time over the hilly San Bartolomé basin far below.

Return to the Los Pechos junction and turn left on the GC130 for Cruz de Tejeda. The northern hills reappear. After 1km turn right to the **Museo de Guayere** (∩M), an ethnological museum set in a huge cave. Some 1km from the museum, turn left for 'Ayacata' on the GC600. Descending through pines, you pass the popular picnic area, **Llanos de la Pez** (70.5km ⊼ with barbecues; WC). It's only crowded on Sundays and holidays. Another 2km downhill, you're circling the Presa de los Hornos (73.5km ▣*P*1b), an eye-catching little reservoir set at the foot of wooded slopes. **Roque Nublo★**, the island's landmark (74km ▣), is the 'high point' of Walk 1 (photographs pages 41, 42 and 78-9).

The tiny village of **Ayacata** (77km), buried amidst great boulders and kept fresh by the green of almond trees, rests at the foot of the *cumbre*. Turn left here along the GC60. Use the notes for Car tour 3 (page 27) to make for **San Bartolomé** (88km). At the junction just beyond the town, keep straight ahead (the right fork) along the GC60, towards Fataga and Maspalomas. The road winds down into yet another ravine, the canyon-sized Barranco de Fataga. It's the largest valley on Gran Canaria and known as 'the valley of the thousand palms'. Further south, you'll see why. The village of **Fataga★** (95km ☗) is superbly sited on a hillock of greenery rising up from the *barranco*. Keep to the GC60; as you head towards the sea, this impressive landscape closes in on you, with sheer rock faces towering overhead.

Cane grows along the valley floor where you come upon **Arteara** (100km), with a large parking area just to the right of the road. From here it's a short walk to the intriguing **Guanche cemetery★** shown overleaf, a site which lay unprotected for centuries. Refer to the notes for Walk 19 on page 100 to explore this wonderful setting — a lavish patch of green in a thirsting landscape (*P*19).

The ascent out of this huge ravine is breathtaking (especially if you are on the outside lane … which is where you *should* be!). A fine viewpoint (✕▣) greets you some 4km uphill from Arteara, as you leave the *barranco*. Not far below this *mirador* you come to **Mundo Aborigen★** (M), an outdoor museum with a replica Guanche village.

Ahead the **sand dunes of Maspalomas**★ offer a complete break in the relief. Unfortunately, the massive tourist enclave of **Playa del Inglés/Maspalomas** chokes out most of the view. Despite the crowds, the beach and dunes are definitely worth a stop. Early evening is the best time to see them. To get there, go straight over *all* the San Fernando roundabouts and, once in Playa del Inglés, straight down Avenida Tirajana. From Maspalomas it's an hour's drive along the GC1 motorway back to Exit A in **Las Palmas** (166km).

*Detour:* If you've already seen Maspalomas, and if the vertiginous drive down the Fataga ravine didn't make you jittery, you might enjoy the spectacular 47km return detour up the Barranco de Arguineguín (allow two hours). To get there, make for Arguineguín on the GC500 (do *not* take the motorway; it bypasses the exit you want). One kilometre *before* Arguineguín, turn right on the GC505 for 'Cercados de Espino'. When you reach Cercados de Espino keep straight on for 'Presa de Soria', below towering valley walls with a surprising amount of greenery. Soria (✕ ☎), 22km uphill, basks in the heights of this impressive gulch, overlooking an equally impressive reservoir. A five-minute stroll down to the dam wall (*P*18a; Walk 18), where you

can peer over the edge, will either leave you in awe or terrified. The valley has become a jagged vertical defile. The asphalt continues for another 1.5km, before reverting to track. Follow it for about 1km, then park by a fork in the road and use the notes on page 13 (*P*18b) to reach one of the best picnic spots on the island, high above the dam.

*Guanche cemetery near Arteara (Picnic 19)*

# ● Walking

This book covers most of the best walking on Gran Canaria, enough to keep even the most energetic rambler happy for a full month. There are walks for all ages and abilities, from short strolls to mammoth hikes.

Admittedly, many of the hikes are linear and tough (due to the nature of the terrain) — or long (to cater for those travelling by bus). *If you have a car,* many easier options are possible (see 'Motorists' below). *Use the book to improve your own rambles.* I've indicated where routes link up on the walking maps, and the fold-out touring map shows the general location of all the walks. One word of caution: *never try to get from one walk to another on uncharted terrain!* Only link up walks by following paths described in these notes or by using roads and tracks; don't try to cross rough country *(extremely dangerous)* or private land.

*There are walks in the book for everyone:*

**Beginners**: Start on the walks graded 'easy', and be sure to check all the short and alternative walks; some are easier versions of the more difficult hikes. **You need look no further than the picnic suggestions** on pages 8-14 to find enough easy walks for a fortnight's holiday.

**Motorists**: Almost every walk is suitable (see 🚗 symbol under 'Access'), and many can be done as circuits. In some cases, it will be far easier to leave your car at the start or end of a walk and begin or end by bus, as the full circuits can be far more strenuous. Otherwise, look at the short and alternative walks for easier suggestions.

**Experienced walkers**: If you are used to rough terrain and have a head for heights, you should be able to tackle *almost* all the walks in the book, taking into account, of course, the season and weather conditions. Please follow the route as described in the book, and if you have not reached one of my landmarks after a reasonable time, return to the last 'sure' point and start again.

**Experts**: A couple of walks are potentially very hazardous, and these are recommended for experts only — those of you who can clamber like goats along precipitous edges and across scree. You will always be properly clothed, shod, and equipped. You will also know how to take compass readings, 'read' the terrain and the weather signals, and you will not panic when surrounded by thick fog.

# Guides, waymarking, maps

**Guides** are not easily found on Gran Canaria, but your nearest tourist office may be able to help you contact one (you will not *need* a guide for any walk in this book).

Thanks to EU funding (which has already been invested in restoring the old *caminos reales**), work is taking place to bring **signposting and waymarking** up to 'Euro' standards (as has already happened on some of the other Canary Islands). There are three types of waymarking (some of which you will see on your walks):

- *Red and white* waymarks indicating GR routes ('Grandes Recorridos': long-distance footpaths);
- *Yellow and white* waymarks indicating PR routes ('Pequeños Recorridos': short trails of up to six hours);
- *Green and white* waymarks indicating SL routes ('Senderos Locales': local trails, up to about 10km long).
- For all these routes, right-angled stripes indicate a 'change of direction; an 'X' means 'wrong way'.

Where we have information about trail numbering, we have have added it to our maps. *But some signs and waymarks may still be haphazard or non-existent on the ground.*

The **maps** in this book (scale 1:50,000) have been very greatly adapted from Spanish military maps dating from the 1990s, using notes made in the field. Many maps, some produced by local councils, are available on the island.

# Where to stay

If you plan to do a lot of walking, and if you will rely on local buses for transport, it is most convenient to stay in **Las Palmas**, a vibrant city and the island's cultural capital. But with excellent bus connections from the south to the interior, you can do many walks from a sun-drenched base in the **Playa del Inglés/Maspalomas/Puerto Rico** axis, where most tourists stay. Or ... why not divide your time between Las Palmas and the south?

If you have your own transport, the well-dispersed *casas rurales* (country cottages) make mouth-watering bases; see, for instance: www. ecoturismocanarias.com, www. grantural.com, and www.naturacanarias.com. Or visit the island's main portal, www.grancanaria.com: click on 'Where to stay' for links to a huge choice of accommodation — cottages, rural hotels, guest houses and the like.

---

*Old stone-laid trails built just after the Conquest, to link isolated villages with the coast; they were financed by the king, hence the name *caminos reales* (the king's roads). The regional government has issued packaged leaflets about them, called *Caminos Reales de Gran Canaria*. These should be available in island bookshops. Although in Spanish, they contain good route maps. See also www.grancanaria.com.

# What to take

Don't attempt the more difficult walks without the proper gear. For each walk in the book, the *minimum* equipment is listed. Where walking boots are required, there is, unfortunately, no substitute: you will need to rely on the grip and ankle support they provide, as well as their waterproof qualities. For all other walks wear stout lace-up shoes, preferably with thick rubber soles that grip on wet or slippery surfaces.

You may find the following checklist useful:

walking boots (which must be broken-in and comfortable)
waterproof rain gear (outside summer months)
long-sleeved shirt (sun protection)
windproof (zip opening)
plastic plates, cups, etc
mobile (the emergency number is 112 throughout the Canaries)
spare bootlaces
sunhat, sunglasses, suncream
torch, whistle, compass
up-to-date transport timetable (see page 7)
plastic bottle with water purifying tablets
long trousers, tight at the ankles
first-aid kit
knives and openers
warm fleece
extra pair of socks
plastic groundsheet
small rucksack
insect repellent

Please bear in mind that I've not done *every* walk in this book under *all* weather conditions, and I may not realise just how hot — or wet — some walks might be. The sun may be your worst enemy. It's tempting to walk in shorts and to forget that, with the sun behind you, the backs of your neck and legs are being badly burned. **Always** carry a long-sleeved shirt and long trousers to put on when you've had enough sun, and **always** wear a sunhat on bright days. In hot weather, take your lunch in a shady spot. *On the other hand, always take warm clothing on mountain walks — it can be very cold on the cumbre!*

# Dogs — and other nuisances

**Dogs** will be the only real nuisance on your walks. They're usually small and noisy, but the sight of a stick sends then scurrying. However, if you do a lot of walking on the island you are bound to meet at least one unfriendly monster, rightly guarding his territory. Throwing stones and *threatening* dogs with sticks is more likely to provoke an already wary dog. Modern technology's answer is the 'Dog Dazer', an ultrasonic dog deterrent. It does no harm to the dog, is very effective (I've had a 98% success rate with it) and is convenient to carry. For details and price see www.sunflowerbooks.co.uk.

There are **ticks** on the island; I've never encountered any, but some correspondents have. **Hunters** may startle you with bursts of gunfire, but they present no other worries. They come out in force on weekends and holidays … always trailed by yapping dogs. Give chained **billy goats** a wide berth; they don't like intruders! Other than that, you've no other pests to worry you on Gran Canaria — there are no poisonous snakes or insects.

# Weather

You needn't be a meteorologist to understand the basic weather patterns on Gran Canaria. Below I outline the four winds that influence the weather and mention some other interesting facts. I hope this information will help you plan your excursions.

The most important wind on the island is the *alisio*, the trade wind. It flows in two currents: the upper current, from the northwest, is warm and dry; the lower current, from the northeast , is wet and cool. The *alisio* drapes a cape of white cloud over the north and northwest of the island for much of the year. This cloud cover hovers between 600-1500m (2000-5000ft). Since the *cumbre*, the central massif, is for the most part well over 1500m, it blocks the clouds from moving over into the south, where clear and sunny days prevail most of the year. In June and July, the cloud cape covers the north and northwest of the island most of the time. But this is not as bad as it may at first appear! The days are still pleasant for walking, with sunny intervals, and, on the heights, you'll be above the clouds. Still, November and January are the best walking months in the north, with nearly half the days free of the *alisio*.

Two winds could really put a damper on your day: the *southwesterly wind from the tropics* and the *northwesterly wind from the Pole*. The tropical wind, recognised by its high, uniform layer of cloud, brings strong gales and torrential rains. It hits the whole island. Fortunately, this wind is very rare. The Polar wind (it strikes infrequently, and only between October and April) breaks through the *alisio*, bringing thunderstorms and cold winds. It can carry some very cold weather, especially at the higher altitudes, where snow may fall. On Gran Canaria, snowfalls are a rarity. The duration of this bad weather is usually two or three days.

A complete change of weather comes with the fourth wind that concerns us — the *sirocco*, sometimes called *el tiempo del sur*. This is a hot wind coming from the Sahara. It won't cause you any trouble, except with photography!

It brings a haze, caused by very fine particles of sand. It is at its worst at the higher altitudes; near the sea the atmosphere can be quite fresh. The *sirocco* is generally a summer wind, lasting three or four days. It's good, but hot, walking weather. Farmers love the *sirocco* ... because rain usually follows!

So as you can see, the weather should not affect your walking. If it's bad in the north, just head south. But remember: this is a small island, susceptible to rapid changes in weather. *Always set off on your walks prepared for the worst, especially in the mountains!*

## Spanish for walkers

In the tourist centres you hardly need to know any Spanish at all. But once you're out in the countryside, a few words of the language will be helpful, especially if you lose your way

Here's an (almost) foolproof way to communicate in Spanish. First, memorise the few short key questions and their possible answers, given below. Then, when you have your 'mini-speech' memorised, always ask the many questions you can concoct from it **in such a way that you get a 'sí' (yes) or 'no' answer.** *Never* ask an open-ended question such as 'Where is the main road?' Instead, ask the question and then *suggest the most likely answer yourself.* For instance: 'Good day, sir. Please — where is the path to Soria? *Is it straight ahead?*' Now, unless you get a 'sí' response, try: '*Is it to the left?*' If you go through the list of answers to your own question, you will eventually get a 'sí' response — probably with a vigorous nod of the head — and this is more reassuring than relying solely on sign language.

Following are the two most likely situations in which you may have to practise some Spanish. The dots (...) indicate where you will fill in the name of your destination. Ask a native speaker to help you with the pronunciation of these phrases and place names (approximate pronunciation of place names is given in the Index).

### Asking the way

**The key questions**

| English | Spanish | pronounced as |
|---|---|---|
| Good day, sir (madam, miss). | Buenos días señor (señora, señorita). | **Boo**-eh-nos **dee**-ahs, sen-**yor** (sen-**yor**-ah, sen-yor-**ee**-tah). |
| Please — where is | Por favor — dónde está | **Poor** fa-**vor** — **dohn**-day es-**tah** |

| the road to …? | la carretera a …? | la cah-reh-**teh**-rah ah …? |
| the footpath to …? | la senda de …? | lah **sen**-dah day …? |
| the way to …? | el camino a …? | el cah-**mee**-noh ah …? |
| the bus stop? | la parada? | lah par-**rah**-dah? |
| Many thanks. | Muchas gracias. | **Moo**-chas **gra**-thee-as. |

**Possible answers**

| *English* | *Spanish* | *pronounced as* |
| is it here? | está aquí? | es-**tah** ah-**kee**? |
| straight ahead? | todo recto? | **toh**-doh **rec**-toh? |
| behind? | detrás? | day-**tras**? |
| to the right? | a la derecha? | ah lah day-**reh**-chah? |
| to the left? | a la izquierda? | ah lah eeth-kee-**air**-dah? |
| above?/below? | arriba?/abajo? | ah-**ree**-bah?/ah-**bah**-hoh? |

**Asking a taxi driver to return for you**

| *English* | *Spanish* | *pronounced as* |
| Please — | Por favor — | **Poor** fah-**vor** — |
| take us to … | llévanos a … | l-**yay**-vah-nos ah … |
| and return | y volver | ee vol-**vair** |
| for us at* | para nosotros a* | **pah**-rah nos-**oh**-tros ah* |

*Point out the time on your watch when you wish to return.

Inexpensive phrase books, such as those published by Berlitz, are very valuable aids, especially since they give easily-understood pronunciation hints. You can also choose other 'key phrases' from them.

# Walkers' checklist

The following points cannot be stressed too often:

■ **At any time a walk may become unsafe** due to storm damage or the havoc caused by bulldozers. If the route is not as described in this book, and your way ahead is not secure, *turn back*.

■ **In the winter** many mountain and *barranco* walks may be very wet and hazardous.

■ **NEVER walk alone.** Four is the best walking group: if someone is injured, two people can go for help, and there will be no need to panic in an emergency.

■ **Do not overestimate your energies** — your speed will be determined by the slowest walker in your group.

■ **Transport** connections at the end of a walk are vital. Don't rely on calling a taxi from a remote location — it is much better to book a reliable driver in advance.

■ **Proper shoes or boots** are a necessity.

■ **Mists** can suddenly appear on the higher elevations.

■ **Warm clothing** is needed in the mountains; *even in summer,* take some along in case you are delayed.

■ **Compass, whistle, torch, first-aid kit, mobile** weigh little, but might save your life.

■ **Always take a sunhat with you**, and in summer a cover-up for your arms and legs as well.

- A **stout stick** is a help on rough terrain and may discourage an unfriendly dog (see also 'Dogs', page 35).
- **Extra rations** must be taken on long walks.
- **Read and re-read** the important note on page 2 and the Country code below, as well as guidelines on grade and equipment for each walk you plan.

## Country code for walkers and motorists

Experienced ramblers are used to following a 'country code', but tourists who take up walking on holiday may unwittingly cause damage, harm animals, and even endanger their own lives. On Gran Canaria especially, the rugged terrain can lead to dangerous mistakes.

- **Only light fires** at picnic areas with fireplaces. Stub out cigarettes with care.
- **Do not frighten animals.** The goats and sheep you may encounter on your walks are not tame. By making loud noises or trying to touch or photograph them, you may cause them to run in fear and be hurt.
- **Walk quietly through all hamlets and villages**, and take care not to provoke the dogs. Ignore their barking and keep your walking stick out of sight. Remember, it is only to be shown to an unchained, menacing dog. (See also note about 'Dog Dazers' on page 35.)
- **Leave all gates just as you find them**, whether they are at farms or on the mountainside. Although you may not see any animals, the gates *do* have a purpose; they are there to keep goats or sheep in (or out of) an area. Here again, animals can be endangered by careless behaviour.
- **Protect all wild and cultivated plants.** Don't try to pick wild flowers or uproot saplings. Leave them for others to enjoy. They will die before you can get them in water, in any case. Obviously fruit and other crops are someone's private property and should not be touched. *Never walk over cultivated land*.
- **Take all your litter away with you.**
- **DO NOT TAKE RISKS!** This is the most important point of all. Do not attempt walks beyond your capacity, and do not wander off the paths described if there is any sign of mist or if it is late in the day. **Do not walk alone**, and *always* tell a responsible person *exactly* where you are going and what time you plan to return. Remember, if you become lost or injure yourself, it may be a long time before you are found. There are no organised mountain rescue services, but in the case of an emergency use your mobile to ring 112 (the standard European emergency rescue

number). On any but a very short walk near villages, be sure to take your mobile — as well as a compass, torch, whistle, first-aid kit, warm clothing and extra water and high-energy food.

# Organisation of the walks

The 26 walks in this book are grouped in four general areas: the centre, off the *cumbre,* the south, and the northwest. You might begin by considering the fold-out touring map inside the back cover. Here you can see at a glance the overall terrain, the road network, and the general location of all the walks. Quickly flipping through the book, you'll also find that there's at least one photograph for each walk.

Having selected one or two potential excursions from the map and the photographs, look over the planning information at the beginning of the walks. Here you'll find distance/hours, grade, equipment, and access. If the grade and equipment are beyond your scope, don't despair! *There's almost always a short or alternative version of a walk* and, in most cases, these are far less demanding. If it *still* looks too strenuous for you, turn to pages 8-14 for a good selection of easy 'picnic walks'.

When you are on your walk, you will find that the text begins with an introduction to the overall landscape and then quickly turns to a detailed description of the route itself. The **large-scale maps** (all reproduced at 1:50,000) have been specially annotated and, where space allows, set out facing the walking notes. Times are given for reaching certain points in the walk. Note that these times *include only brief stops* to catch your breath or look at the view. *Do* allow for lunch and photography breaks, or any stops of indeterminate length. And *do,* please, **check your pace against mine** on one or two shorter walks before setting off on any strenuous hikes. This is **vital** where bus connections are infrequent.

Below is a key to the symbols on the walking maps:

| | | |
|---|---|---|
| ▬▬▬ expressway | ↔ spring, tank, etc | ⛪ church |
| ▬▬▬ main road | P picnic suggestion (see pages 8-14) | † shrine |
| ▬▬▬ secondary road | | ⊞ cemetery |
| ▬▬▬ track | 🕶 best views | ⌓ picnic site with tables |
| ----- path, steps | ⚐ danger! vertigo! | |
| 6→ main walk | 🚌 bus stop | ⚡ pylon, wires |
| 12→ alternative walk | 🚗 car parking | ⫘ map continuation |
| ▬▬▬ watercourse, pipe | ■ specific building | i visitor centre |
| 2→ walk in watercourse | I I dyke; gate | ☼ ∩ mill; cave |
| | – 400 – altitude (metres) | ⍥ rock formation |

# Walk 1: LA CULATA • ROQUE NUBLO • LA CULATA

See map on reverse of the touring map; see also photographs of Roque Nublo on pages 4 and 78-79

**Distance/time:** 6.3km/4mi; 3h

**Grade:** strenuous; overall ascent of 400m/1300ft, steep descent back to La Culata. Not suitable in wet weather. PR GC 60 throughout

**Equipment:** walking boots, sunhat, long-sleeved shirt, long trousers, warm fleece, warm jacket, gloves, raingear, picnic, plenty of water

**Access and return:** 🚌 18 (Timetable 20) to/from La Culata or 🚌 303 (Timetable 9) to San Mateo, then change to 🚌 18 as above; journey time with either service about 2h). Or 🚗: park in La Culata.

**Short walk:** Circuit round Roque Nublo (4km/2.5mi; 2h). Relatively easy, with an overall climb of 200m/650ft. Not suitable in wet weather. Access by 🚗: park in the parking area beside the GC600, north of Ayacata. Pick up the main walk at the 1h05min-point. When the main walk turns off left to descend to La Culata (at the 2h10min-point), keep straight ahead, back down to your outward path. Descend to the Ayacata road, 30min away. (The Presa de los Hornos, a good five minutes up the road from the car park, is worth a short stroll (Picnic 1b); this is *included* in the 2h allowed for this walk.)

**Alternative walk:** La Culata — Roque Nublo — Ayacata (6.4km/4mi; 2h40min). Strenuous, with a steep ascent of 400m/1300ft and a descent of 300m/1000ft. Equipment, access as main walk. Return from Ayacata on 🚌 18, then 🚌 30 if going on to Las Palmas (see second return bus option for Walk 15 on page 87). Follow the main walk for the first 1h40min (to Roque Nublo), then retrace your steps to the point where the Roque Nublo path leaves the Ayacata road. Just before reaching the parking area for Roque Nublo on the GC600, turn right on another path and follow it down to the road. Turn right and, two minutes down the road, take a path left through a gap in the roadside guard rail. Five minutes later, rejoin the road and turn left. After 85m/yds, your path continues to the right. Remain on the main path. After descending for 10 minutes, pass between a couple of dwellings and join a private lane. On reaching the road again, turn right for 20m/yds, then go right to rejoin the path. Coming to a lane, turn right for 12m/yds, then turn left on a path down to Ayacata, a few minutes away (50min after leaving the Roque Nublo path). PR GC 60 throughout

**Alternative circuit for motorists:** GC600 — La Culata — Mirador de Becerra — GC600 (12km/7.4mi; 4h35min). Very strenuous, with overall ascents/descents of about 800m/2600ft. Equipment as main walk. Access by 🚗 as *Short walk* above. Pick up the main walk at the 1h05min-point and follow it to the end. Just before the bus stop in La Culata, ascend a concrete path on the right with green handrails (1h55min). Cross a road and continue up a cobbled path until you meet a narrow road.

*Roque Nublo*

Follow this to the right for a few minutes, then fork left up a lane. This peters out into a path, passes a spring (Picnic 8) and rises to the GC150 road. Turn left to the Mirador de Becerra (3h05min), then pick up Alternative walk 7 at the 1h20min-point (page 61) to return to your car.

Mysterious Roque Nublo, a monolith of rock balancing on a table-top mountain, is Gran Canaria's proud landmark. Beside it, only a few metres away, stands a replica in miniature. Whether seen from far away or nearby under its spell, it's easy to understand why this eye-catching rock was sacred to the Guanches. The panorama from this ancient sanctuary captures the veins in the landscape, sharp-edged ridges segmenting the valleys below. Be prepared for company on your visit to this rock: this is the most popular hiking route on the island.

From the car park/bus stop in **La Culata**, **start out** by following the road uphill, past the BAR ROQUE NUBLO. Just beyond a HOUSE BUILT ON CONCRETE COLUMNS, with a swimming pool (**5min**), turn right on a path stepping down into a *barranco*. Once across the stream bed, continue straight uphill. On coming into a hamlet, pass the end of a road and continue up beside a stream bed; it soon becomes another boulder-strewn *barranco*. Now on a cobbled trail, climb past the last houses and keep left at a fork (**15min**). The fork to the right will be your return route. A second fork follows; again keep left. A few minutes further uphill, you enjoy a bird's-eye view of La Culata from a rocky nodule (Picnic 1a). The path winds uphill amidst pine trees.

The path bends right, crosses a dry STREAM BED (**40min**) and climbs towards the GC600 Ayacata road. Deep volcanic tones, mauves and maroons, ooze out of the bare eroded escarpment. Approaching the ROAD

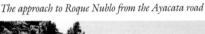

*The approach to Roque Nublo from the Ayacata road*

*Presa de los Hornos (Picnic 1b)*

(**1h05min**), turn right on the path to Roque Nublo, just on the north side of the road. *(The Short walk starts and ends here.)* The surrounding terrain is a mass of round rocky abutments pierced by occasional fingers of rock. *Tabaiba* and yellow-flowering *retama* brighten the slopes in the spring. The monolith becomes increasingly impressive as you near it. Barely 15 minutes up the path, you pass a turn-off to the right *(the Short walk and Alternative walks descend this path.)* On reaching a CREST (**1h30min**) a small pine-studded basin appears below, swallowed up by these enormous abutments. (On the return, you will descend to the left here, down into this basin.)

Enjoy the superb view over to El Teide on Tenerife, then clamber up the rocky ridge on your left, where more astounding views unfold, straight down onto Ayacata. Now ascend the two gigantic platforms of rock, which lead you up to the once-sacred **Roque Nublo** (**1h40min**). It's a magnificent sight: these two rocks, father and son, stand soldier-straight against a backdrop of deep blue sky. You look straight down into the Barranco de Tejeda, seaward bound, in its attempt to cut the island in two. To its left lies the cleft of the Barranco del Corilla, narrower and more severe. Tejeda, a sprawl of white houses, lies on the gentler inclines below on your right.

Soak up the view, then return to the junction less than 10 minutes back. Descend to the right, into the basin below. *(But those doing the Alternative walk keep left.)* At a junction 10 minutes downhill, turn right. When the path forks again, some 10 minutes later (**2h10min**), keep left. *(But for the Short walk keep right, to continue straight ahead.)* Descending into a side-valley behind La Culata, you have a good view across the tail of the Barranco de Tejeda. Soon the inclines are bright green with *tabaiba*. The impressive descent takes you down to a derelict building; keep to the left of it. When you rejoin your outward path (**2h45min**), follow it downhill to the left, soon coming back into the hamlet. Descend for another 10 minutes, back to **La Culata** (**3h**).

# Walk 2: TEJEDA • BARRANCO DE TEJEDA • CASAS DE LA UMBRIA

**Map on reverse of touring map**
**Distance/time:** 9km/5.6mi; 3h 55min (motorists add 1h)
**Grade:** *expert* (see page 33), with a steep descent of 450m/1500ft and an overall ascent of 700m/ 2300ft). You must be sure-footed and have a head for heights: for 1h10min the walk follows a narrow water channel above the valley floor (see photographs right and page 26). This involves squeezing past rock faces and, in a few stretches, the sides of the *canal* have broken away. Don't attempt the walk in wet weather, and if the *canal* has any water in it, abandon the walk!

**Equipment:** walking boots, sun-hat, long trousers, long-sleeved shirt, warm fleece, windproof, raingear, picnic, plenty of water; stick to beat back brambles along the *canal*.

**Access and return:** 🚌 to/from Tejeda or 🚐 18 (Timetable 20) to Tejeda; journey time about 2h; return on the same bus line from Casas de la Umbría (also called Las Moradas de Tejeda), back to base or back to your car. Or 🚐 303 (Timetable 9) to San Mateo, then change to 🚐 18 (Timetable 20); return to San Mateo on 🚐 18 and change to 🚐 303.

*Photo: viaduct along the* canal

Discover the Barranco de Tejeda, where you'll be lucky to see another hiker. A *canal* leads through the depths of this *barranco*, along the narrow winding valley floor. And if you're lucky a stream will accompany you.

From the bus stop in **Tejeda**, **start out** by walking to the CHURCH shown on page 26. Just beyond it, turn left down a very steep narrow lane flanked by houses and walls overflowing with geraniums. Ignore side-lanes to the left but, when you come to a T-junction (**13min**), keep left. Two minutes later, on a bend, where there is a small hillock in front of you, leave the lane: turn right and follow a path round the left-hand side of this hill. After a minute, you pass above a water tank and ignore a path down to the left. A path joins from the right. Keep right at the next fork. A good five minutes from the lane, below a small shed, ignore a path to the right. Now it's down, down, down. The rough gravel path winds down through almond covered hillsides into the verdant **Barranco de Tejeda**.

When a *canal* cuts across your path (**35min**), turn right for a few metres/yards and, brushing against trees, climb *into* the water channel. This *canal* will be your 'path' for over an hour, while you remain in the floor of the *barranco*. Be prepared to encounter many obstacles (landslips, drops in the level, broken-away edges, etc), where you must scramble off the *canal* and then climb back in.

The *canal* quickly penetrates a 'tunnel' of cane and, not

far along, leads over a FIRST VIADUCT (see photograph opposite). Beyond it, you leave the water channel briefly and follow a track. A small farm of gardens and orchards terraces the valley floor here. Beyond a SECOND VIADUCT, and just before a large round WATER TANK, go up the concrete track towards a white house. Where the track swings sharp right, take a path down into a small *barranco*. At the bottom, follow the right bank of the little stream for about 100m/yds, then go left to cross a THIRD VIADUCT (**50min**). The stream bed is crammed full of cane and the hillsides above lightly wooded with tired old almond trees. The FOURTH VIADUCT has a huge hole and is impassable: you must scramble off the *canal,* cross the *barranco,* rise up the other side and walk along to where you can rejoin the *canal.* Then cross a FIFTH VIADUCT (**1h20min**).

About 25-30 minutes later, *watch for* a CONCRETE RAMP leaving the *canal* (**1h45min**)*;* ascend the faint path opposite it, climbing above the water channel. (Note: if you come to a second ramp 10m/yds past the first one, you have overshot the turn-off.) A couple of minutes up the path, just above a shed, keep left at a fork.

Round the hillside, always keeping to the main path. The abandoned hamlet of La Higuerilla comes into sight, on the far side of a small valley with overgrown gardens. At the confusion of paths that follows, keep left on the clearer path and, a minute later, come to a lone, partly-renovated building. Circle to the right of the building, and then turn left uphill to a TRACK (**2h**). This track is your way out of the valley: a tough climb lies ahead.

The village set high in the valley wall opposite is Artenara. The very prominent crag rising out of the ridge above is Roque Bentaiga. After less than one hour up the track, join the GC607 (**3h**) and turn left. But before doing so, admire the craggy cave-pitted ridge above to the right, the **Cueva del Rey**, the once-great seat of the Guanche kingdom (see photographs page 26). Meeting the GC60 at **Casas de la Umbría** (**3h55min**), hail down your bus. But if no bus is due for a while, you could just walk back down the GC60 to Tejeda (about 3.5km; 1h).

*Rock pools in the Barranco de Tejeda*

## Walk 3: CASAS DE LA UMBRIA • EL ESPINILLO • LA SOLANA • EL CHORRILLO • EL CARRIZAL • DEGOLLADA DEL ASERRADOR

Map on reverse of touring map; see also cover photograph

**Distance:** 14km/8.7mi; 6h15min (or 19km/12mi; 7h30 if you walk back to Casas de la Umbría)

**Grade:** strenuous and long, with an ascent of about 750m/2450ft and descent of 600m/2000m. But suitable for any fit person who is sure-footed and has a head for heights. PR GC 80 throughout

**Equipment:** walking boots, sunhat, fleece, windproof, raingear, picnic, water

**Access and return:** 🚐 to/from Casas de la Umbria (also known as Las Moradas de Tejeda) or 🚌 18 (Timetable 20) to Casas de la Umbría; return on the same bus line from the Degollada del Aserrador, back to base or back to your car. Or 🚌 303 (Timetable 9) to San Mateo, then change to 🚌 18 as above; return to San Mateo on 🚌 18 (Timetable 20) and change to 🚐 303.

The island's most beautiful villages lie in a delightful string on this route, set deep in far-flung valleys. There are magnificent vistas to enjoy and, if that isn't enough, you'll have most of this tranquillity all to yourself.

From **Casas de la Umbría, start out** along the road to Roque Bentaiga and Cueva del Rey. Then take the first left turn, towards Roque Bentaiga and El Espinillo. Three minutes along this road (**10min**), turn left to descend a path bordered by a stone wall. The path bends right to traverse a dry rocky hillside. Straggly old almond trees and low scrub share the slopes. Crossing a crest, you descend into the deep, severe **Barranco del Corilla**. Tall aloes flank this old *camino,* which crosses the ROAD TO EL ESPINILLO. Roque Bentaiga (see photographs pages 14 and 48), an important religious site during the Guanche epoch, dominates the right-hand side of the valley.

Joining the road again (**40min**), you descend into **El Espinillo**, a pretty, well-cared-for hamlet with bright terracotta roof tiles. These small, once-neglected mountain villages have been brought back to life by families returning and converting their ancestral homes into weekend retreats. When the road ends, continue on the path from the right-hand side of the parking area, keeping straight downhill (the right-hand fork). A deep *barranco* slides away on the right; abandoned fields lie on the left.

La Solana is the next village to come out of hiding. It sits on the terraced nose of a ridge above the valley floor. The path zigzags down a steep craggy ridge. Enter the *barranco* bed (**1h05min**) and follow it downhill for 50m/ yds, then fork left on a path. Ignore a faint fork to the left. Wind your way through large rocks and boulders, cross a

*Taginaste*
(Echium
decaisnei)

*Cerrajón*
(Sonchus
ortunoi)

*Palo sangre*
(Sonchus
tectifolius)

*Retama*
(Spartocytisus
supranubius)

*Peorera*
(Andryala
cheiranthifolia)

low crest and recross the bed of the *barranco*. Climb into **La Solana** (**1h20min**), which overlooks a bib of gardens and orchards decked with palms. The shady plaza with nearby bar makes a good rest stop.

Take the path between the bar and the plaza. It winds down the hillside behind the bar, on the edge of the *barranco*. After three minutes' descent, turn right on another path, to pass behind a handful of houses. Luxuriant garden plots flank the way. After three minutes more, just beyond a path to the left, cross a side *barranco* and bend left. Ten minutes from La Solana, you descend to the GC607 (**1h 30min**), and turn left for El Chorrillo, a tiny village perched precariously on the crest of a high narrow ridge.

Entering **El Chorrillo** (**1h 55min**), climb the path immediately up to the right. It's worth looking into the first alley to the left to take in an exquisite village scene. Leave the village along the *second* alley to the left. Then turn right, quickly joining a cobbled path. Citrus groves terrace the top of the ridge, from where a superb panorama over the whole valley unfolds. After five minutes' climbing from the village (just beyond a small side-*barranco*), you meet a fork: climb up to the left here. A minute later, keep left at another fork.

Back in scrub, a steep path takes you up and over the escarpment — to where an even

Senecio sp.

*Codeso* (Adeno-
carpus foliolosus)

*Margarita*
(Argyranthemum)

*Valo*
(Plocama
pendula)

*Sea fennel*
(Crithmum
latifolium)

*Top: the road to El Espinillo, with Roque Bentaiga to the right. Bottom: entering El Carrizal ... where you'll find my favourite bar.*

more desolate valley awaits you. Traces of crumbled stone walls and the cloak of dead and dying almond trees speak for themselves. Soon a view unfolds directly across to the Vega de Acusa (Walk 26), the flat-topped tongue of ridge shown on page 4; it stands out from the vast cauldron of deep ravines.

Mounting the crest of a ridge (**2h40min**), El Carrizal — the next village en route — appears not far below, set on the steep *barranco* wall. The ravine wall opposite thrusts up into a blade of rock, peppered by a number of cave houses in its higher reaches. The forested hills of Pajonales fill in the backdrop.

The path heads left to descend to El Carrizal. Coming into the upper half of the village, you catch sight of the striking Embalse del Parralillo set deep in the gorge below, its green waters accentuating the bare rock walls of Barranco de la Aldea. Join a village road and turn right. Then turn left on a descending path, down to the parking area and plaza at **El Carrizal** (**2h55min**). Time to refuel, and where better than in my favourite bar (behind and to the right of the church), its courtyard crammed with pot plants.

Follow the road out of the village, to a fork. Keep right and, after a minute (just past a couple of houses), go left up a cobbled path. Climb past gardens buried amongst prickly pear and enter a narrow valley, its walls thickly matted with vegetation. At the third *barranco* crossing, walk upstream and relocate the path 30m/yds along. The path turns right out of the stream bed and climbs to rejoin the El Carrizal road (**3h50min**). Turn right. After several minutes you come to a spectacular roadside viewpoint down into the plunging Barranco de Siberio, with a couple of totally isolated outposts in its depths.

From this viewpoint, continue along the road a few metres/yards and then take the path that continues straight off the road and follows the edge of the cliff. The way turns sharp left up a faded stony path to join the road again five minutes later. Continue uphill along the road. Just below the first house in **El Toscón** (**4h15min**), the road skirts a rounded loaf-shaped crest of rock. Scramble up it, to a lone belfry and intriguing cross for another magnificent view over the Barranco de Siberio (Picnic 3).

*Aeonium nobile*

Stay on the road to just past the LAST HOUSES (**4h35min**), built into a bulging crest of rock. Then, 30m/yds beyond a roadside *fuente* (water tap) on the left, turn right on a path which descends into the **Barranco del Toscón**. The hillside falls away steeply below this path. After 10 minutes your path enters a stream bed of bare rock. Follow the bedrock downhill for 25m/yds, then you will see your path again, going left across the hillside. The whole landscape is sprinkled with long-abandoned almond trees.

*Ranunculus cortusfolius*

After barely 20 minutes from the road, just after crossing the *barranco* bed, the way suddenly bends right. Half a minute later, at a fork, keep left. The winding path leads up a hillside littered with crumbled stone walls. Tall aloe stalks punctuate the hillside. When you again rejoin the ROAD (**5h 50min**), turn right and follow it for 25 minutes to the GC60 at the **Degollada del Aserrador** (**6h15min**), where you can flag down the bus (or walk back to your car\*).

*Red-flowering tabaiba* (Euphorbia atropurpurea)

*Canary bellflower* (Campanula canariensis)

*Vinagrera* (Rumex lunaria)

\*Follow the GC60 north for about 35 minutes, to a left bend (just before the KM9 marker). Take the signposted track to the right, quickly rising to the **Cruz de Timagada**. Walk 8 is off to the right here, but go *left* (there *may* be a sign: 'PR GC 80'). Striding along this ridge, you have the fine view shown on pages 64-65. When the path meets a track, turn sharp left down to the GC60. Casas de la Umbría is not far to the right.

# Walk 4: FROM CRUZ DE TEJEDA TO ARTENARA

**Map begins overleaf; ends on page 121; see also photograph page 1**

**Distance/time:** 8.5km/5.3mi; 2h30min

**Grade:** easy descent of 600m/1970ft, after a steep initial ascent of 200m/650ft. But you must be sure-footed and have a head for heights for the detour to the cliff-edge caves at the 1h15min-point (and do *not* take this detour if it is misty; it is potentially dangerous in damp weather).

**Equipment:** walking boots, sunhat, long trousers, long-sleeved shirt, warm fleece, warm jacket, gloves, raingear, water, picnic

**Access:** 🚌 18 (Timetable 20) to Cruz de Tejeda (journey time 2h40min) or 🚌 303 (Timetable 9) to San Mateo, then change to 🚌 18 as above; journey time about 2h)

*To return:* 🚌 220 from Artenara (Timetable 7)

Yeou'll be thrown into a hiking mood as soon as you get off the bus. From the rim of the enormous craggy basin at Cruz de Tejeda the world is yours: sharp ridges, bold peaks, and views in every direction. Cliff-top caves (alas sealed off by iron railings) set high on the brink of the Tejeda Valley offer an interesting detour. Artenara, your destination, is an artists' dream. Its little white houses poke their faces out of the richly-hued wall of the *barranco*. And in this mountainside lies a masterpiece, a chapel carved into the rock.

**Start the walk** at **Cruz de Tejeda** (Picnic 4). Follow the GC150 due north (the road to the right of the *parador,* as you face it). After 200m/yds, on the left side of a large parking area, take the trail to the left (sign: 'PARQUE RURAL EL NUBLO'). (Walk 6 takes the trail to the right here.) After a few minutes, circle to the left of a water tank. Then ignore a path to the left. A steep ascent now follows.

*The path to the cave chapel shown on page 1, seen from Artenara*

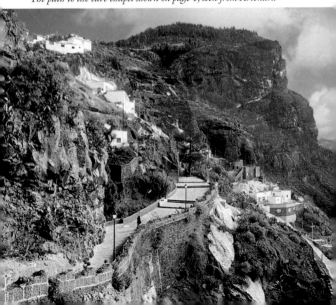

You'll be captivated by the far-reaching views. Two rocks stand out in this rugged terrain: Roque Nublo (Walk 1) in the distance, to the left, and Roque Bentaiga on the opposite ridge. Tejeda spreads across two ridges descending into the valley below. The path runs down to the road to Los Pinos de Gáldar, where the *mirador* **Degollada de las Palomas (35min)** gives you another chance to absorb this wild panorama.

Continue along the path behind the shelter at the *mirador,* heading up into a patchy veil of pines. Soon the path widens into a track. On meeting a FORESTRY TRACK (**55min**), turn left. *(Walk 5 turns right downhill here.)* After 10 minutes, just beyond a turn-off to the right, you arrive at a junction. There's a good look-out point on the hillock 100m/yds to your right: on a clear day El Teide on Tenerife seems to rise straight up out of the sea.

Returning from the look-out point to the junction, continue along the main track, below the cross. After 10 minutes, you're walking past huge boulders balancing on the lip of the ridge. The **Cuevas del Caballero (1h15min**; Gentleman's Caves) are on the other side of these rocks, facing Tejeda. For a detour to visit them, take the small track (later a path) leading between the rocks. Several fenced-off caves lie in this vertiginous perch. What a view to wake up to — straight out over the Barranco de Tejeda and, to the right, the flat-topped Vega de Acusa.

Back on the main route, you come to a fork in the track (**1h50min**): keep left, to continue straight ahead. Ignore a turn-off to the left but, a couple of minutes later, take a short-cut to the right. Rejoining the track, leave it after a minute: descend a stone-laid path on the right (now referring to the map on page 121). Then, at a fork, keep left downhill. Cross a narrow road (**2h15min**), and climb the wide path on the left. As you mount the ridge, Artenara comes out of hiding ... bit by bit.

Now, as you descend, quaint little dwellings peep out of the face of the mountainside. Cacti, *taginaste* and *valo*, threaded with geraniums, have transformed the severe rock-face into an enchanting garden. After a few minutes, you come out onto the neat paved area shown opposite, rich in volcanic reds and purples. The Tejeda Valley lies before you. Visit the tiny chapel shown on page 1: carved into the rock, it lies a little way along to your left. Then follow the path out to the road. Walk 500m/yds down the road to the centre of **Artenara (2h30min)**. The bus leaves from just below the plaza.

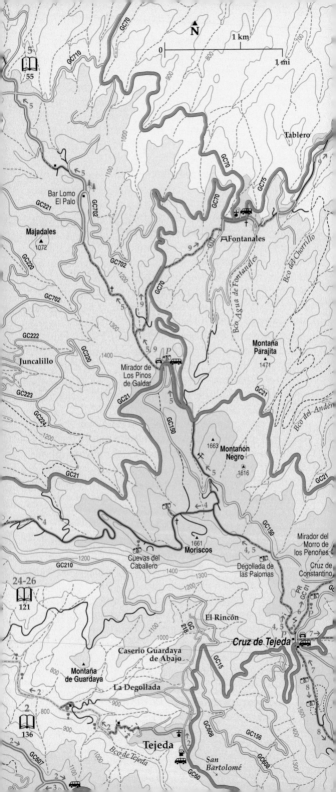

Firgas

Osorio
▲ 968

Arucas

Las Madres

GC305

GC30

9

GC307

La Laguna

GC21

Los Llanos

Teror

GC432

GC21

Las Palmas

9 →

6 →

GC213

Caserón

9

Monagas

PR GC 01

Las Rosadas

El Alamo

GC42

Montaña Lentisco
1077 ▲

GC305

Mirador Balcón de Zamora

Casas de la Vuelta

600

Valleseco

GC21

6

Las Cuevas

Arbejales

700

Bar El Lomo

PR GC 01

Montaña Moreno
1055 ▲

GC424

6 →

Los Naranjeros

Ermita del Corazón de Jesús

Lanzarote

Madrelagua

GC214

6

Bco del Chorquillo

Las Calderetas
P

Cuevas de Corcho

GC230

Presa de Arinez

GC423

800

GC421

GC422

San Mateo →

GC42

GC400

800

900

Bco de las Lagunetas

Mirador de Mña Cabreja

GC230

GC154

Las Lagunetas

San Mateo

12 →

7 →

PR GC 10

la Mina

7

La Lechuza

GC15

GC15

Mña Troya
▲ 1107

Bco de

GCH14

GC41

Valsequillo

1300

7, 8

PR GC 10

12 →

Bco de Higuera

Montaña la Caldereta
▲ 1184

136

12

136

12

1200

1300

1400

Cueva Grande

## Walk 5: CRUZ DE TEJEDA • MIRADOR DE LOS PINOS DE GALDAR • SAUCILLO • GUIA

Map begins on pages 52-53, ends opposite; see also photographs pages 10 and 68

Distance/time: 16km/10mi; 5h20min

Grade: easy, but long, with an ascent of 200m/650ft and descent of 1500m/5000ft. Not recommended in bad weather.

Equipment: walking boots, sunhat, long trousers, long-sleeved shirt, warm fleece, jacket, gloves, raingear, plenty of water, picnic

Access: 🚌 18 (Timetable 20) to Cruz de Tejeda (journey time 2h40min) or 🚌 303 (Timetable 9) to San Mateo, then change to 🚌 18 as above; journey time about 2h)

To return: 🚌 103 or 105 from Guía to Las Palmas (Timetables 2, 3; departs 10min after leaving Gáldar; journey time 45min)

Shorter walks
1) **Cruz de Tejeda — GC220** (9km/5.6mi; 3h20min). Access/equipment/grade as main walk (descent: 650m/2130ft). Follow the main walk to the CG220 (bus stop); 🚌 106 departs for Gáldar 15.55 *Mon-Sat*.
2) **Mirador de los Pinos de Gáldar — Guía** (11.5km/7mi; 3h50min). Easy descent of 1300m/4250ft. Equipment as above. Access: 🚌 220 from Las Palmas or Teror to the Mirador de los Pinos de Gáldar (Timetable 7). Follow the main walk from the 1h30min-point to the end.

This superb walk stands apart from all the others on the island: it's easy strolling, sea breezes keep you cool on the hottest of days, and it crosses verdant grassy slopes, where you'll see shepherds out with their flocks of sheep. Sagging stone walls squaring off the hillsides add to the rural charm. Dark gravelly slopes, the scars of volcanic activity, provide a brief interlude during your descent.

**The walk begins** at **Cruz de Tejeda**. Follow Walk 4 (page 50) to the FORESTRY TRACK (**55min**). Here turn right and descend. The island's northern slopes unfold, as they fall and merge into undulating hills. Grass and ferns cover the hillsides in this pine-dominated landscape. Some 200m/yds downhill, ignore a turn-off to the right. Three minutes later, where the track bends to the left, take a minor grassy path descending to the right. Then pick up the parallel minor track, and follow it down to the road.

Cross the road and clamber over the roadside embankment to continue down the gravel track skirting to the left of **Montañón Negro**. Fine, coal-coloured gravel, sprinkled with delicate purple- and white-flowering *alhelí*, provides a brief interlude in the landscape. Chestnut trees begin appearing amidst the pines. After a few minutes' descent, you pass through an old quarry.

On reaching another road (GC21; **1h15min**), turn left. Within 15 minutes you reach the **Mirador de los Pinos de Gáldar** (**1h30min**; Picnic 5). What a view! Gentle farmed hills amble down to the sea. Small ravines drain the landscape as they wind their way seaward. In the distant northeast, Las Palmas and La Isleta can be seen; just below you, sunk deep in the hillside, lies the crater of Los Pinos de Gáldar.

To continue, skirt the guardrail on the left of the viewpoint, and walk down between the old stone walls below the car parking area. These walls are a strong feature in the immediate landscape. Slide your way down the steep gravelly slope. El Teide can be seen rising on Tenerife, behind the wooded heights of Tamadaba. After 15 minutes, the two walls end at a junction of paths, by a sign, 'MONUMENTO NATURAL TAÑON NEGRO' (**1h45min**). Turn left. *(Walk 9 goes right at this junction.* Then turn right immediately, continuing along the top of the crest. A faint path takes you round the left-hand side of the now-grassy ridge. The pines are fading quickly … as is your path! Just keep alongside the wall, crossing grassy slopes.

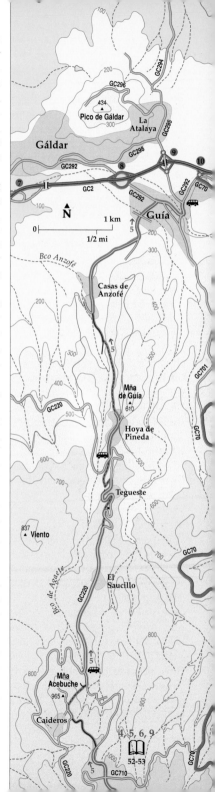

When a FENCE blocks the way (**1h 55min**), head left, walking alongside it. After a minute, you pass the CROSS shown on page 10, standing in front of a stone enclosure. Three minutes further down you leave the fence, and another stone wall continues in its place. Cross in front of the wall and keep it on your left. Barely five minutes later, the path leaves the wall and bends to the right round the hillside, to reach the GC702. Turn right on this road. Much of the countryside is fenced off by enormous aloes. In the past, these plants served a dual purpose: their stalks were used to hedge fields and pen livestock, while rope, halters, whiplashes and the like were made from the fibre extracted from their leaves.

Walk along the road to the BAR LOMO EL PALO (**2h25min**) and, 150m/yds beyond it, turn left down a country road; a small wood stands off to the right. Some three minutes downhill, take the first track on the left, with a field of *escobón* (white flowering tree broom) off to the right. After two minutes, at a fork, keep right along a drive and pass below a house with noisy dogs. Continue on a path running straight off the drive. You pass some shepherds' pens and descend to a wide road. Follow it all the way down the ridge, through strips of cultivation and pasture. Agaete and Puerto de las Nieves appear through the valleys to the left and the volcanic cone of Pico de Gáldar rises to the right.

Cross a ROAD (GC710; **2h50min**) and keep straight on downhill, now referring to the map on page 55. A little over five minutes later, ascend a track to the left (waymarking: two yellow dots on a wall at the right). After rounding another fresh green valley, you pass behind the upper houses of **Caideros**, set on the edge of the Barranco de Agaete. Keep right through both junctions here. Then, 35m/yds beyond the second junction, turn right down a path that descends to the right of **Montaña Acebuche**. Five minutes downhill, join a driveway and, when you come to a narrow road, turn left to the GC220 (**3h20min**; *Shorter walk 1 ends here*). Turn right and walk through **Saucillo** (**3h35min**), where the restaurant serves up a fine

mutton stew (*oveja en salsa*). The sprawling village of
Gáldar comes into view, spread round the base of Pico de
Gáldar. Ten minutes from Saucillo, where the road bends
right, turn left on a path (paved at first). Rejoin the road
for a minute, then turn left on a drive beside a house.

A wide path continuing off the drive leads you down
to **Tegueste**, a small village built into and around a crest,
with a number of caves of prehispanic origin. Returning
to the ROAD (**3h55min**), turn left. After five minutes, by
a large lay-by on the right, turn left through a gap in the
roadside railings, onto a path. After 50m/yds, keep right
at a fork. When you meet the main road again, cross it and
take the minor road at the right of a BUS SHELTER.

Passing through **Hoya de Pineda** (**4h15min**), a small
village tucked away on the slopes of Montaña de Guía,
keep downhill to the left. When the road ends, continue
on a path descending to the right, above houses and below
a high rock face. Your view reaches out over the severe
Barranco Anzofé to Gáldar and its banana plantations.
After 10 minutes, turn right on a track. A few minutes later
you enter **Casas de Anzofé** and tar comes underfoot.
Follow the road over a bridge, pass through a junction,
and come to the GC290. Turn right here, then go left at
the T-junction in **Guía** (**5h20min**). The bus stop is two
minutes to the right, just past the CENTRO MÉDICO.

## Walk 6: CRUZ DE TEJEDA • CALDERETAS • LAS ROSADAS • TEROR

**See map pages 52-53**
**Distance:** 12km/7.4mi; 3h20min
**Grade:** easy-moderate, with overall ascent of 200m/650ft and descent of 900m/ 3000ft. You must be sure-footed and have a head for heights. Avoid in bad weather. PR GC 01 throughout
**Equipment:** walking boots, sun-hat, long trousers, warm fleece,

windproof, gloves, rainwear, picnic, water

**Access:** 🚌 18 (Timetable 20) to Cruz de Tejeda or 🚌 303 (Time-table 9) to San Mateo, then 🚌 18 as above (see details on page 50)
*To return:* 🚌 216 from Teror to Las Palmas (Timetable 8); journey time 45min
*Above: Cortijo de Calderetas*

This walk makes a pleasant introduction to the bucolic charms of the north. You're bound to meet shepherds and their flocks as you descend from the roof of the island, with expansive panoramas before you all the way.

**Start the walk** at **Cruz de Tejeda**. Follow the GC150 due north (the road to the right of the *parador,* as you face it). After 200m/yds, on the left side of a large parking area, take the signposted *camino real* rising to the right ('PR GC 01; TEROR 12 KM'). (Walks 4 and 5 use the trail to the left.) You pass below an electricity sub-station. Already the views distract you (Picnic 6a). Behind you, monolithic Roque Nublo (Walk 1) balances on a table-topped ridge. The island's summits are draped in woodland. The farming village scattered across the valley below is Las Lagunetas. Fuerteventura lies on the distant horizon. Once you cross the GC150 ROAD at **Cruz de Constantino** (**20min**), your ongoing path is almost all downhill.

You descend through pine woods to the lush pastures of the **Barranco del Charquillo**. After 10 minutes you reach the **Mirador del Morro de los Peñones** (**30min**), an outcrop with a fine vista over the northern hills, to Las Palmas and La Isleta. Villages shelter amongst these waves of hills. Below the *mirador*, cross the *barranco* and seven minutes later, at a fork, take the higher, left-hand path. Coming down to makeshift animal pens and a water tank, follow a track downhill to the GC21 at **Cuevas de Corcho** (**50min**). Pockets of chestnut trees dot the hillsides.

Turn right along the road, cross the road signposted to Tejeda, and then ascend a hillside path on the right. On crossing the ridge, you come upon the shepherds' domain. If you meet any flocks up here, please give them the right of way. Always keep to the clear main track; many animal trails cross it. You recross the ridge and soon a view unfolds down into Las Calderetas, one of the island's more recent volcanoes. Its grassy slopes and chestnut groves make it one of the most picturesque spots on the hike (Picnic 6b). On the crater floor lies the traditional Canarian farmstead shown opposite, the **Cortijo de Calderetas**. Circling to the right of the farmstead, and just above the crater floor, walk to a WATER TROUGH (**1h10min**). Just below this, turn right on a farm track.

Leaving the crater, there's a view over the farming community of Lanzarote, set along a shallow valley cultivated from wall to wall. Your way becomes a concrete lane; when it bends sharp left, keep straight ahead on a minor track. Rejoining the GC21, turn right, soon passing the old village washing area, on the left. Keep right at a first fork ('MADRELAGUA') and left at a second ('LAS PALMAS'). After some 15 minutes you reach BAR EL LOMO (**1h40min**) … but it's been closed for several years.

Just beyond the bar and the last house, where the road veers left, continue straight ahead on a grassy track which runs along the edge of the **Barranco del Charquillo Madrelagua**. At the start, ignore a path on the right to a garden but, not far along the track, turn right on a smaller path down into the valley. As the *camino* winds down to the valley floor, ignore a number of side paths. It's a beautiful valley, part wild, part cultivated. The path narrows considerably and then joins a road. Turn left. After a few hundred metres/yards the road ends at two charmingly restored houses. Go between them and take a footpath along the valley floor through healthy citrus groves. Cross a FOOTBRIDGE and ascend steps to a ROAD (**2h**) on the other side of the valley. The few cottages hidden amongst the orchards and gardens here are called **Los Naranjeros**.

Turn left on the road, to continue down the valley. Soon the way roughens to a track, the plots diminish, and the rocky valley walls close in. Ignore a turn-off to the left. After 15 minutes on this track, you round a bend and come into the tiny hamlet of **Las Cuevas**. Immediately before a garage on the right, turn left down a signposted path. The route takes you down into the scrub-congested valley floor: cross it (**2h25min**) and walk round the hillside below a high stone wall. Ignore a path to the right and then one to the left.

After 10 minutes, you pass through the strung-out village of **Casas de la Vuelta**, each little house occupying its own little crest. Keep straight on to join the end of a road in **Las Rosadas**. Follow this road to the right. Ahead lies Teror, a large sprawling village stretching across a gentle pause in the valley walls.

After five minutes, you rejoin the GC21 ROAD (**2h 50min**). Two minutes downhill (50m/yds beyond a bus stop sign), turn right down a steep rough concrete lane (Camino Lugar Cuesta Los Estanques). At a T-junction, keep right. A beautiful stroll between houses and gardens follows. Keep straight down to rejoin the main road, and turn right. After three minutes, you can take a short cut to the left, to cut off a bend in the road. Entering **Teror** (**3h20min**), keep left at an intersection. After a couple of minutes, cross straight over the next intersection. Continue until you reach a PETROL STATION; the BUS STATION is next to it.

*La Culata (near Alternative walk 7)*

# Walk 7: LAS LAGUNETAS • BARRANCO DE LA MINA • MIRADOR DE BECERRA • CRUZ DE TEJEDA • LAS LAGUNETAS

Map on reverse of touring map; photograph opposite (Alternative walk)

**Distance:** 8.5km/5.5mi; 3h25min

**Grade:** strenuous, with an ascent/descent of 400m/1300ft. You must be sure-footed and have a head for heights. Only recommended for experienced, confident hikers: the path is somewhat difficult to follow at times. The walk is only suitable on cloudless, fine days; in any other weather it is potentially dangerous, owing to the rugged steep terrain. Note that the *cumbre* can be very cold and windy.

**Equipment:** walking boots with good grip are *essential;* sunhat, long trousers, long-sleeved shirt, warm fleece, jacket, gloves, raingear, picnic, plenty of water

**Access and return:** 🚌 18 (Timetable 20; journey time 2h50min) or 🚌 303 (Timetable 9) to San Mateo, then change to 🚌 18 as above; journey time about 1h50min); alight/reboard at the Las Lagunetas turn-off. Or by 🚗: park off the side of the GC15 about 500m west of the Las Lagunetas turn-off, at a parking bay in front of a shop on the left (ask for permission first: 'Poor fah-**vor**, kee-see-**ay**-ra-mohs ah-par-**kar** ah-**kee** kon soo pair-**mee**-soh.')

**Alternative walk: Las Lagunetas — Barranco de la Mina — Mirador de Becerra — Presa de los Hornos — La Culata** (8.5km/5.5mi; 3h35min). Grade as main walk, plus a steep, gravelly descent of 370m/1200ft to La Culata. Access and equipment as above. Return from La Culata as Walk 1, page 41. *Highly recommended* for experienced walkers. Follow the main walk to the Mirador de Becerra (1h20min). Turn left (south) on the GC150 road here, then take a path off to the right just past the *mirador*. After five minutes, at a fork, ascend to the left. *(Walk 8 goes right here.)* After 30min more (1h55min) at a fork, keep right to continue straight ahead. After five minutes cross a track, and two minutes later cross the track again (where a right turn leads to a 'Zona de Acampada'). Continuing straight ahead, enter the stream bed (or walk alongside it). When you reach a track, follow it to the right. After five minutes, at a junction, turn right along a very wide path. A minute later, turn left and, after 25m/yds, take the cobbled path descending alongside a stone wall into a valley (which *may* be signposted PR GC 60). Cross the dam wall of the Presa de los Hornos and climb to the viewpoint above (2h45min). Turn right down the GC600 road and, after five minutes (by a parking area), you reach the turn-off to Roque Nublo and La Culata. Follow the Roque Nublo path a short way, then descend to the right for La Culata, 45min downhill. Follow this clear path all the way down and, when you meet a road, descend left to a turning area and the bus stop.

T his walk offers stunning views and a spectacular little ravine, the Barranco de la Mina, wedged into the shoulder of the *cumbre*. Hidden away in this *barranco* are waterfalls the like of which you won't see anywhere else on Gran Canaria. Later in the walk, when you reach the roof of the island, grassy meadows come under foot. But to avoid disappointment, be prepared to do a different walk altogether, if you find the *cumbre* covered in cloud or bad weather suddenly threatens.

**Start the walk** at the TURN-OFF TO LAS LAGUNETAS. Walk west along the GC15 towards Cruz de Tejeda. Just after crossing the cascading stream in the **Barranco de la Mina** (**10min**), turn left up a chained-off lane hemmed in by high rocky walls (signpost: 'PR GC 02, BECERRA'). Willows fill the floor of the ravine below you, and strips of terracing step the inclines above. After three minutes, the lane ends. Keep straight ahead on a path. Just beyond the last building, keep right at a fork.

The ravine walls are matted in vegetation, and spongy green moss clings to the rock. It's a cool spot, green and damp — quite unexpected on this island. From now on you will encounter vertiginous sections of path at regular intervals. Ignore all paths to the left until, five minutes from the last fork, you come to another fork: descend to the left here, to cross the stream under a canopy of trees and bushes. A narrow path clinging to the sheer hillside leads you up the opposite bank. Small cascades appear through the undergrowth. An extravaganza of vegetation covers the valley walls, including aloes, *aeoniums*, tree broom, prickly pear and *sonchus*.

Five minutes uphill from the stream, at an important FORK (**25min**), continue to the right, following the stream. *(The walk will soon return to this point and continue along the branch to the left.)* A couple of minutes further on, a short stretch (2m/yds) of vertiginous path takes you into a tiny canyon above a high waterfall. Penetrating this tiny canyon for another 40m/yds, you come to an even more impressive waterfall in a cool, salubrious setting. *Do not* be tempted by the dangerous path climbing to the left out of the *barranco* here; *please go back* three minutes to the fork and turn right uphill. The path bends sharp left and passes between two boulders. Just above the boulders, the path bends right again. Two minutes later, when you join a path ascending from the right, keep left, still climbing.

This section of the hike is confusing, as there are a number of paths and short-cuts. Basically the route continues up the hillside; you should be keeping the ravine itself down to your right. There are occasional PR WAYMARKS and some blue paint dots. Ignore paths off to the right until, about 10 minutes uphill from the boulders, you come to a stretch of open hillside above abandoned plots. Keep right here, rounding the hillside.

A spectacular sight awaits you: another good-sized waterfall plunges down into the ravine below. The path is narrow here, so stop before you admire the view! Edging around the face of the escarpment, you come onto a lush flat GRASSY AREA wedged between the *barranco* walls (**1h**), the perfect place to get your breath back (but watch out for broken glass lying around). From the edge of the cliff there's a fine view out through the valley to Las Palmas. Willows crowd along the valley floor.

Go straight across the flat area for a minute, when you will see a cave on your left. Climb up beside it. You reach an old water channel and two more caves. Turn right here on a clear path climbing along the hillside, with chestnut groves lying below you. The path is narrow and steep. Soon you pass below half a dozen houses concealed amidst trees on the valley wall opposite. Water pipes and a sluice in the valley floor mark the source of the stream.

Still ascending, shepherds' trails lead you up the *barranco*. You cross the valley floor several times. A little over five minutes above the hamlet, the path climbs onto a terrace (you will have left the *barranco* bed by now). Walk to the left of a derelict building waymarked with a blue arrow and join a track which ascends the right wall of the *barranco* to the road above. After a few minutes ignore a track to the left; two minutes later, be sure to look into the intriguing caves cut into the hillside on the left side of the stream bed.

Just below another derelict building, 10 minutes up the track, you cross the road on the *cumbre* (GC150) and arrive at the **Mirador de Becerra** (**1h30min**). From here a superb panorama sweeps over the deeply-gouged Caldera de Tejeda. *(The Alternative walk leaves the main walk here by turning taking a path just past the mirador.)*

From the *mirador* follow the GC150 to the right, but then climb a cobbled path to the left. After five minutes, when you rejoin the road, follow it to the left for five minutes, then pick up your ascending path again, on the left. Joining a track, follow it to the left. Between two enclosed properties it reverts to path and you reach the top of the *cumbre*. Take another rest here to admire a view stretching across all the *barrancos* slicing into the centre of the island.

On the descent, the path curves left downhill, and you follow it to the GC15 at **Cruz de Tejeda** (**2h10min**). Turn right and, after 40m/yds, descend a path at the right of a line of tourist kiosks, into pines and chestnut trees. A few minutes downhill, you cross the GC15 and head down between terracing. The sprawling village of Las Lagunetas comes into view bit by bit. *Retama* and *codeso* patch the inclines, and herds of goats graze the herbaceous valley walls. When you rejoin the GC15 (**2h30min**) turn right. After 10m/yds turn left down a concrete path, cross a driveway and keep straight on, winding past houses. This pretty rural setting overlooks Las Lagunetas, set amidst a patchwork of fields covering the valley floor. The path widens into a lane. On reaching the last house, turn sharp left on a path, then turn right towards the GC15. You join the road just above the friendly BAR PERERA. Turn right for 50m/yds, then fork left down a driveway. Turn right off the drive on a path running between high concrete walls.

Walk down the crest of a ridge through a cluster of houses. Stepping down to the GC15 again, turn right. After 15m/yds, take the path to the left. Cross a track to the right of an ELECTRICITY SUB-STATION and go down the track below it. Pick up the path again at the next house. Just after coming onto the end of a concrete drive, at a T-junction with a tarred lane, turn left and continue straight down a ridge edged by houses. When the lane ends, turn left on a path beside the stream bed. Some 50m/yds down the floor of the *barranco*, turn left, cross the bed, and join a track. This takes you to a small road (**3h05min**), where you turn right.

Climbing to another *barrio* (quarter) of **Las Lagunetas**, you pass a turn-of-the-century house on the right. At the T-junction above it, turn right and, a minute later, ascend the cobbled path on the left. The village square, where you'll find a couple of friendly bars, lies to the left. The GC15 and BUS STOP (**3h25min**) are a couple of minutes along to the right. Or continue along to the shop to find your car.

*View across the Caldera de Tejeda, a 10-minute detour on Walk 8*

## Walk 8: CRUZ DE TEJEDA • LA CULATA • TEJEDA

**Map on reverse of touring map, see also photographs pages 26, 60**
**Distance:** 11km/7mi; 3h20min

**Grade:** fairly easy ascent of 150m/500ft, followed by a long descent of 550m/1800ft. You must be sure-footed and have a head for heights. Not suitable in bad weather, and note that it can be very cold and windy.

**Equipment:** walking boots, sunhat, fleece, windproof, long trousers, gloves, thick socks, raingear, picnic, water

**Access and return:** 🚐 18 (Timetable 20) to Cruz de Tejeda or 🚐 303 (Timetable 9) to San Mateo, then change to 🚐 18 as above; journey time about 2h); return on the same bus from Tejeda.

Short and sweet, this walk gives you spectacular views from the roof of the island. Descending to La Culata, a charming country village where time seems to have stood still, you enter a beautiful valley gushing with water.

**Start the walk at Cruz de Tejeda:** take the cobbled path to the right of the HOTEL DEL REFUGIO (as you face it). Heading though *codeso*, *retama* and chestnut trees along the grassy *cumbre*, you'll have to watch out during the first minute for irresponsible hikers answering 'calls of nature'. After a few minutes, at a fork, ascend to the left. Already a striking panorama unfolds over the Barranco de Tejeda and its tributaries, to the distant greenhouses of San Nicholás. Tenerife rises above the clouds. Tejeda, on the slopes below, comes out of hiding. The two monumental rock landmarks to the south are Nublo and Bentaiga.

Soon the path skirts a FENCED-OFF ESTATE on the left (**15min**). Keeping straight on, join a track and follow it until it turns sharp left. Here, take the path to the right. Now your view encompasses the northern hills, speckled with white houses; sheep graze the surrounding pastures.

Dropping down to join the GC150, turn right. After five minutes, just beyond a dirt track to the right, turn right

on a concrete lane ascending to a house. Take the path to the left of the house. Rejoining the road, turn right to the **Mirador de Becerra** (**40min**). Enjoy the stunning view; La Culata, the small clusters of houses set along the wall of the Tejeda Valley below, is your next destination. Your path leaves from the right-hand side of the road just past the *mirador*. Keep right at a fork five minutes down. *(Alternative walk 7 climbs to the left here).* Pine trees run down the inclines and, in summer, bright yellow-flowering *retama* is a magnificent sight here. You pass a SPRING (**1h**; Picnic 8); this corner makes a superb picnic spot, with its chestnut trees and small streams bouncing down the hillside.

You join a LANE (**1h20min**), from where there is a superb view of Roque Bentaiga, Montaña Altavista and El Teide — all in a row. After two minutes, turn right down a narrow road. A few minutes later, turn left down shallow steps onto a cobbled path. After a minute or so, when the path meets a concrete track at a house, turn left; turn right at the junction and go under a wire frame with climbing plants. Then turn immediately left downhill on a concrete path with green handrails, looking into gardens, courtyards and animal pens. Step down to the centre of **La Culata** (**1h35min**). To the right is a parking area and bus stop.

Leaving the village, descend steps from the parking area down to the valley floor. Cross the FOOTBRIDGE, turn right and ignore a path to the right. Meeting a track at a T-junction, follow it to the left uphill for 10m/yds, then turn right uphill on a driveway. Go past the house; your path continues straight ahead. Ignore a path to the right and cross a tributary. A steady ascent follows, during which you ignore a path to the right. The slopes are wooded with *escobón*, *tabaiba* and almond trees.

Eventually (**2h15min**) you come to the turn-off right to Tejeda. Roque Nublo stands directly above you here. (Before going down to Tejeda, you might like to go *left* here. A 10-minute detour would take you via the Cruz de Timagada to the crest of the ridge, the fine viewpoint across the Caldera de Tejeda shown on pages 64-65.)

Some 20 minutes down the Tejeda path, you pass above some gardens, go straight over an intersection, and join a farm track. When this track bends sharp left (below an abandoned building), take the (faintly vertiginous) path to the right, round the hillside. Descend to a track in the floor of the *barranco* (**3h**) and turn left, joining the Tejeda road (GC60). Turn right for 15 minutes, to the BUS STOP by the PETROL STATION in **Tejeda** (**3h20min**).

## Walk 9: MIRADOR DE LOS PINOS DE GALDAR •
## FONTANALES • LA LAGUNA • TEROR

**See map pages 52-53**       **Distance/time:** 13km/8mi; 4h25min

**Grade:** quite strenuous, with an overall ascents of about 450m/1475ft and descents of 900m/3000ft. You must be sure-footed and have a head for heights. Not suitable in bad weather, and it can be cold and windy!

**Equipment:** walking boots, sunhat, long trousers, long-sleeved shirt, warm fleece, jacket, raingear, picnic, plenty of water

**Access and return:** 🚌 220 from Las Palmas or Teror to the Mirador de los Pinos de Gáldar (Timetable 7; journey time up to 1h45min). Or 🚗 to Teror, then 🚌 220 to the *mirador*. Return on 🚌 216 from Teror to Las Palmas (Timetable 8; journey time 45min) or by 🚗.

Dipping in and out of valleys high in the northwestern hills, this walk trails through villages full of charm and unfrequented by tourists. Flocks graze the lush valleys walls in these endearing quiet corners of the island.

**Start out** at the **Mirador de los Pinos de Gáldar**, described on page 54. Following the same route as Walk 5, skirt the guardrail on the left of the viewpoint, and walk down between the old stone walls below the car parking area. Slide your way down the steep gravelly slope, hedged in by bright yellow *retama*. The two walls end at a junction of paths, by a sign 'MONUMENTO NATURAL TAÑON NEGRO' (**15min**). Turn right here. *(Walk 5 goes left.)*

Your *camino* descends into the wooded valley to the right. Climbing up the far side, you cross a track. This very picturesque valley is a mixture of pastures and light stands of pine trees. Climb to a ROAD (GC70; **30min**) and turn left. Five minutes along, turn right on a path flanked by low stone walls. It takes you down into another valley, scattered with chestnut groves. Surmounting a crest, you pass amidst eucalyptus, white-flowering broom, ferns and bright yellow-flowering *Hypericum grandifolium*.

Cross a small *barranco* (**55min**) and join a concrete lane, below a picnic area. Follow the lane downhill. After a few minutes, when you meet the GC70, turn right. Cross a bridge and enter **Fontanales**. After 300m/yds, opposite a bus shelter, turn right up steep CALLE LA MONTAÑETA. After a minute you pass a small shrine built into a tree trunk on the right. Some 300m/yds along this road, just past house number 7, turn left up a wide track (concreted at the outset). (Keeping straight ahead here would take you back to the *mirador* — an ascent of 500m/1650ft). The track turns right behind the house and narrows as you head northeast up this quiet valley, terraced with vegetable plots.

Where the path widens out, ignore a track coming in from the left; keep straight on for 100m/yds to a small country road, the Camino del Lomo el Marco (**1h 15min**). Turn left and, after 80m/yds, turn right on a narrow lane through a rural landscape of cultivated hills and valleys, dotted by houses. Descending the crest of a ridge, you pass through a hamlet. When the main lane swings left down to the road, continue straight ahead on a gravel track (Camino El Tablero), following the crest. The volcanic mound protruding out of the hills ahead and slightly to the right is Osorio. Two deep ravines lie to the right, and the countryside takes on a rugged appearance.

Joining the GC75 in **Tablero** (**1h35min**), turn right and, after 100m/yds (by a bus shelter), turn right again up a concrete lane, Calle Corvo. Far-reaching views of cascading ridges run away on either side of you. Keep right at a fork, remaining on the top of the crest, ignoring tracks to both left and right. The Barranco del Corilla, below to the right, and the Barranco de la Virgen (further away to the right) carve great ravines into the landscape. Houses and garden plots vie for space on the tops of the crests.

Ten minutes from the GC75, ignore a turning to the left followed by a large enclosed estate. A steep descent follows, during which you ignore a minor track to the

right. Keep to the edge of the *barranco*. When you join a narrow tarred ROAD (**2h10min**), turn right, then turn right again immediately on a farm track, passing below house number 37. When the track ends, continue straight ahead on the lower path, descending to the left. An old

*Yellow-flowering* retama *at the Mirador de los Pinos de Gáldar*

paved *camino real* comes underfoot, leading down into the **Barranco de la Virgen**. Traces of the original laurel forest still remain on the ravine walls. In spring, with the *viñátigos*, chestnut trees and oaks in leaf, this *barranco* is an arboreal treat.

Reaching the *barranco* floor, join a road and turn left. Some 75m/yds along, turn right to rejoin the *camino*, descending into the stream bed. Cross the stream bed and ascend to the right, ignoring a fork to the left. Then ignore a minor path to the left. Just past a beautiful old traditional house set amidst trees, keep left at a fork. A very steep climb takes you above a large fenced-in orchard. The path leads onto a track and then a small ROAD (**2h50min**). Continue uphill; cottages cluster atop the ridges; trees abound, and the countryside is verdant and fresh. When the road forks, go left uphill, passing a magnificent old manorial home to the left. Huff and puff up to a road, cross it, and keep straight on up the steep lane opposite, with a fine view over surrounding villages.

Finally, the climb temporarily eases at a T-JUNCTION (**3h20min**). Turn left and, after just 20m/yds (below a wooden cross), turn left on a track. Ignore a track to the left a minute along. Continue round the hillside into a side-valley, passing behind a row of houses, and stay on this track through the charming rustic hamlet of **Monagas**. On meeting a small road, turn right for a few metres/yards, then turn left up a rough concrete lane. Cross a track and keep straight up between old lichen-flecked stone walls shaded by chestnut trees.

Cross the GC30 on your continuing path and, a minute later, go over a junction and continue on a track through an apple orchard. To the left lies a small park with a pond (**La Laguna**). On reaching a road, turn left and, after 100m/yds, turn right to descend to the GC21 (TEROR ROAD; **3h50min**). Cross the road. Teror sprawls across a hillside basin just below. Cross the same road again and then turn right to pass a small building on a *canal*. Cross this watercourse and then turn left. Five more road crossings follow, before a track takes you past a FOOTBALL PITCH.

Join the GC21 in **Los Llanos** and turn right. After 100m/yds, when the road curves right, keep straight down to the left, on the CAMINO DEL CASTAÑO. After five minutes, turn sharp right down CALLE DE LA HERRERIA to the centre of **Teror**. Turn left at a T-junction. The BUS STATION is a couple of minutes ahead, across a junction (**4h25min**). But first explore this charming, unspoilt country town.

**Distance/time:** 8km/5mi; 2h45min

**Grade:** strenuous; for fit and adventurous hikers, even though the overall ascent is only 100m/330ft and the descent 300m/1000ft. You must be sure-footed and have a head for heights. At the start of the walk, above the ruins of the spa, the path is rough, slippery, and vertiginous; scrambling and a bit of climbing is unavoidable. The path down the *barranco* bed to San Andrés is at times hard to follow and involves pushing through stretches of bamboo groves. Do not attempt just after wet weather, as the path is slippery and could be dangerous; in winter you may have to wade for a short stretch.

**Equipment:** walking boots with good grip *essential;* sunhat, warm fleece, long trousers, windproof, raingear, picnic, water

**Access:** 🚌 210 from Las Palmas to Arucas (Timetable 5; journey time 35min). Or 🚍 to San Andrés, then 🚌 213 to Arucas (not in the timetables): departs 08.35, 10.20, 11.55 Mon-Fri, 08.35, 10.20, 12.20 Sat. At Arucas change to 🚌 123 towards Moya (Timetable 6); alight at the Barranco Azuaje; journey time 20min
*To return:* 🚌 105 from San Andrés to Las Palmas (Timetable 3; journey time 25min); or by 🚍

**Short walk: Barranco Azuaje** (3.3km/2mi; 1h20min). Grade, equipment and access as above (ascent/descent of 100m/330ft). To return, arrange in Arucas for a taxi to collect you from the turn-off down in the *barranco*. Or 🚍: heading west from Arucas on the GC300/GC350 (see map), turn down the very rough concrete track on the western side of the Barranco Azuaje. Park 0.3km downhill, near an enclosed spring. Follow the main walk from the ruined spa up to the waterfall and back.

The Barranco Azuaje is crammed full of vegetation, and a little babbling brook keeps you company as you thread your way through trees and bushes to a pretty waterfall. The walk is in two sections: up the *barranco* to the waterfall, and then down it to San Andrés. The abandoned ruins of a once-elegant spa mark the point where the two sections diverge.

Alighting from the bus at the turn-off to the **Barranco Azuaje**, **start the walk** by crossing the BRIDGE and turning left down the second (concrete) track descending to the valley floor. You pass a dirt track forking off to the left; later in the hike you will follow this track to San Andrés. Soon you are following an ebullient stream. This sheer-sided valley is already lush and green. Continuing past an enclosed spring (which is the best place to park for the Short walk), you come to the remains of a colonnaded SPA at the foot of a towering escarpment (**5min**; Picnic 10).

A couple of minutes later the track ends at the start of a defile of rock flooded

*The abandoned spa at the start of the walk*

with vegetation. The next part of the walk is an 'out and back' excursion to visit a pretty waterfall. The air is damp. Follow the path leading into the jungle of *vinagrera, taginaste, verode, Hypericum,* ferns, cane and blackberries. Keep left at a fork below a water tank. Stay beside the stream all the way up. Five minutes after leaving the track, ignore a path to the right to a *galería* (water 'gallery' — a place where water is drawn from the rock through a tunnel bored to a spring). Cross the stream a couple of times. The small clear pools are irresistible in the hot summer months.

A short climb takes you up the right-hand wall of the valley (**30min**). *Take care here: this short stretch is steep, narrow, slippery and vertiginous, particularly if wet!* You descend to the stream again and, passing to the left of an abandoned building, you come upon the prettiest spot in the valley. An enchanting 'wood' of *Hypericum* grows along the valley floor, which is carpeted in clover; the sheer valley walls drip with greenery, and the air is filled with the scent of *Artemisia*.

The final section of this part of the walk is another scramble. Just beyond the wood you have to descend a 3m/10ft-high rock face. Follow the stream bed, soon coming to a beautiful pool by the WATERFALL (**40min**). Some 15m/yds before the falls another scramble leads to a continuing path, but the main walk turns back here. Retrace your steps to the track 300m/yds below the spa building (**1h15min**) and follow it to the right. *(But for the Short walk, head left, back to your car or waiting taxi.)*

Keeping along the valley floor, the *barranco* opens up ahead of you. Garden and banana plots appear stepped high up the steep valley walls. Ignore a track ascending to the left (**1h45min**). Several minutes further along the *barranco* bed, the track dies out and a path continues along the valley floor. You may have to move a wooden fence aside; be sure to replace it: it's used to pen horses in the valley. And don't be surprised to come upon inquisitive

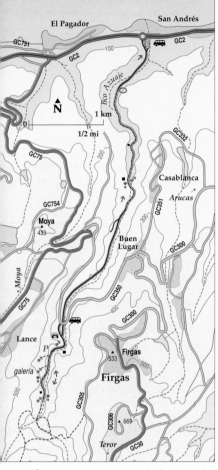

horses in the 'jungle' that follows. Brushing past vegetation, by this time you are floundering over stones. The odd *finca* sits back by the valley walls.

After about 15 minutes, at the edge of a DRY CASCADE (**2h**), it looks as if you can go no further. Cross to the left of the stream bed and walk along a narrow ledge beside a fenced-off *finca* (a fairly vertiginous stretch). After a minute, a gate blocks your way, but you can scramble down the rock embankment and rejoin the path. Back in the *barranco* bed, you now have to push your way through cane. After five minutes, you pass below an abandoned homestead to the left. Prickly pear clings to the valley walls above you.

*Attention is needed* five minutes later, just after the *barranco* curves noticeably to the left. Keep an eye out for a path to the right through the dense vegetation. *Don't* continue along the stream bed — the cane becomes impenetrable. The path leads you up to the left of a garden plot. From here descend to a TRACK (**2h20min**) and follow it out of the valley. Banana plantations terrace the hillsides above the track, and enormous bushes of *taginaste* flank the route. After 15 minutes, you round a bend and San Andrés lies just ahead, with the sea behind it. When you reach the FOOTBALL GROUND at **San Andrés** (**2h45min**), walk on to the main GC2. Turn right and in a few minutes come to the BUS STOP — or walk on to your car.

72

## Walk 11: BARRANCO DE GUAYADEQUE: MONTAÑA DE LAS TIERRAS • CALDERA DE LOS MARTELES • VALSEQUILLO

See map on reverse of touring map

**Distance/time:** 13km/8mi; 4h50min

**Grade:** very strenuous, with an ascent of 500m/1600ft and a descent of 950m/3100ft. You must be sure-footed and have a head for heights. Only suitable in fine weather. The *cumbre* can be very cold and misty.

**Equipment:** walking boots with good grip, sunhat, long trousers, long-sleeved shirt, warm fleece, jacket, gloves, raingear, picnic, plenty of water

**Access:** 🚌 11 from Las Palmas to Agüimes (Timetable 14; journey time 45min), then 🚕 taxi or 🚌 27 to Montaña de las Tierras (not in the timetables; departs *Mon, Wed only* at 08.00; journey time 30min)
*To return:* 🚌 13 from Valsequillo to Telde bus station (Timetable 13; journey time 15min); change to Las Palmas 🚌 12 (Timetable 12; journey time 25min)

**Short walk: Caldera de los Marteles — Valsequillo** (7.5km/4.5mi; 2h40min). Easy descent of 950m/3100ft, but note the vertigo and weather warnings above. Equipment as above. Access: 🚌 to Telde, then 🚕 taxi from Telde to the Caldera de los Marteles viewpoint. Return as main walk. Follow the main walk from the 2h10min-point to the end.

**Alternative walks for motorists** (🚕 to Montaña de las Tierras): Several paths and tracks radiating from the Caldera de los Marteles and Montaña de las Tierras are shown on the map, to enable you to plan some circuits. They *should* be waymarked, but I have *not* done them all myself (the sections I have not done are not highlighted). One possibility is to just follow the main walk to **Las Brucias** and back (8.5km/5.5mi; 2h30min). A popular circuit (15km/9.3mi; 5h40min) uses the main walk ascent to the **Caldera de los Marteles**, then the track south of the *caldera* to the GC130. Just before the bend in that road, turn left on another track and follow Walk 13 to the **Cruz del Socorro**. Then take the track to the left. When this bends sharp left, go ahead on a ridge path. Some 20 minutes along the path be sure to fork left, down the west side of the Barranco de Guayadeque, back to your outgoing route (*the path further east, straight down from Paso Pino Calzados is said to be very overgrown*).

The Barranco de Guayadeque is one of Gran Canaria's lesser-known beauty spots. This narrow craggy defile harbours some of the best Guanche cave finds on the island although, unfortunately, they are not easily accessible.* For the locals, the 'cave-restaurants' alone, set in the precipitous valley walls, are worth the visit. Homeward bound, and more than likely swallowed up in damp swirling mists, you'll be under the magic spell of the Roques de Tenteniguada, great basaltic columns rupturing the valley walls — this hike offers some breath-taking scenery.

On entering **Montaña de las Tierras** (Picnic 11), take

*Entering the *barranco*, be sure to visit the 'Centro de Interpretación de Guayadeque' (open Tue-Sat 09.00-17.00, Sun 10.00-18.00, closed Mon). Some 2.5km further on, in the village of Guayadeque, go up the concrete ramp/steps on the left, just before the chapel. House 17 is open to visitors. All the houses here have been cut out of the rock.

the road to the left for 200m/yds, to the BAR VEGA, where **the walk begins**. (This bar is known for its wine and pork dishes, but expect to pay tourist prices; Restaurant Tagoror, at the entrance to the village, has been painstakingly carved out of the hillside, and it's worth having a drink there just to see the interior.)

Leave the village on the only track out. Rough and dusty, it leads you up the **Barranco de Guayadeque**, completely encircled by towering walls — a corridor of rock opening out to the sea far below. The track curls up through terraced plots, on inclines lightly wooded with fresh green almond trees. From the outset, you're huffing and puffing. The last thing you expect to find up here is more dwellings. But higher up this never-ending ravine more little houses appear on the steep hillsides.

Note the second *barranco* crossing (**40min**). A minute beyond this, by a small cairn on the left, turn left on a footpath and cross back over the stream bed for the third time. Your path ascends between solid stone walls. After two-three minutes, keep right at a fork, then remain on this path all the way up the valley. The inclines are thickly covered in almond trees, with pockets of cultivation on the gentler stretches.

After 10 minutes on the path you cross the stream bed. At this point the path turns sharp left. The remains of a derelict outpost stand above you to the right. Passing the outpost, the path recrosses the *barranco,* then zigzags up to the left. Ignore a minor path to the right, and come to a junction opposite another derelict building (**1h05min**). Here the path turns left uphill and later runs right, to cross terracing. *Escobón* now takes over much of the countryside, hedging the pathway in. Several minutes later, you recross the stream bed. The way then turns left to climb a gravelly slope, now in the company of pine trees. Ascend to **Las Brucias (1h 20min)**, a small pastoral settlement hidden in a coomb high in the *cumbre*.

On reaching a track, follow it straight uphill for a minute. Then, just

*The northern side of the Caldera de los Marteles, on the GC130, before the descent to Tenteniguada.*

after a fenced off *finca* (estate), by a black pipe, turn right up a path signposted 'CAMINO DE LA CALDERA' and waymarked with splashes of white paint. This path turns right along the hillside and takes you behind the *finca*. After a couple of minutes, be sure to turn left uphill on another path, alongside a small *barranco* to the right. Rejoining the track, follow it uphill. The dogs at the first house you pass could wake the dead! Keep your Dog Dazer handy. Another chained guard dog lies in wait at the second house, just above. Climbing out of this quiet coomb, the track passes alongside the **Caldera de los Marteles**. Ignore a track joining you from the left here.

Ascend to the GC130 (**2h**) and turn left (the photograph below was taken nearby). After 10 minutes on the road, the descent to Tenteniguada begins: take the SECOND TRACK (**2h10min**) to the right, opposite the crater and lay-by for the VIEWPOINT. *(The Short walk begins here.)* On a cloud-free day, you set off with a spectacular view. Descend a steep slope into the deep Barranco de la Capellania, lightly wooded in pines. Clusters of small *Aeoniums* hang from moss-covered rock. Some 15 minutes downhill, past some caves, ignore the fork on the right. Continue uphill for two minutes, then take the path to the right (**2h25min**) waymarked with cairns — a shepherds' path through tunnel-like scrub.

Soon the path crosses a crest and turns right along it; a low stone wall runs along the outer edge of the path, where

*Caldera de los Marteles in spring*

the hillside falls away. Ignore a turning to the left (**2h40min**) and then wind down a worn, gravelly shepherds' path through a tunnel of shoulder-high viper's bugloss (*taginaste azul,* absolutely spectacular in March and April). On finally coming out of the clouds, you overlook an immense valley scattered with sprawling villages, orchards and gardens. Fantastic rock formations grow out of the surrounding mountain walls: teetering rocks, giant upthrusts, blades, and pinnacles.

Dropping down onto a CONCRETE LANE (**3h20min**), enter **Rincón de Tenteniguada**, a charming settlement of rustic cottages set in an exuberance of vegetation. After going left for five minutes, turn right along CALLE EL ROQUE GRANDE. Continue straight down to a fork and keep right on CALLE EL GUINDO. At a T-junction with the GC413, turn right. After two minutes (just after rounding a bend), descend a concrete path to the right, which leads down to a road. Follow this downhill, then turn left on CALLE LAS PORTADAS. Keep left at the next two junctions.

You join the MAIN GC41 in **Tenteniguada** (**4h**). If you've worked up an appetite, the lively and popular Las Cañas restaurant lies 100m/yds to the right. To continue, cross the GC41 and keep straight ahead on CALLE SAN JUAN. A few minutes later, ignore a turn-off left. A deep gully, the **Barranco de la Plata**, drops away to the right. Valsequillo lies ahead, set along the brink of this gully.

Keep right all the way to **Las Casillas**, where the road ends. Continue by taking the path to the right through a scattering of eucalyptus. Entering a wild corner of countryside, you wind down into the gully to the right. A path joins from the left. Cross the gully and follow a track uphill to the right. Passing through a hamlet, ignore a turning to the right. Cross the MAIN GC41 and descend to the valley floor — where there's rubbish everywhere (watch out for broken glass). A short way along the *barranco* bed, leave it by climbing up a wide stony path into the houses on the embankment above. Then walk back up to the GC41, cross it, and enter **Valsequillo** (**4h50min**). Rejoin the GC41 below the church. Follow it to the right downhill for three minutes, to find your BUS SHELTER on the right.

# Walk 12: CRUZ GRANDE • ALTO DEL CAMPANARIO • PICO DE LAS NIEVES • SAN MATEO

Map on reverse of touring map; see also photograph pages 8-9

**Distance/time:** 15.8km/9.8mi; 5h55min

**Grade:** strenuous, with an ascent of 750m/2460ft and descent of 1150m/3775ft. You must be sure-footed and have a head for heights. The walk can be *very cold and potentially hazardous;* recommended for experienced walkers, and only in fine weather. Alto del Campanario sits atop precipitous crags, and in cloudy conditions the path to and from the summit is difficult to follow. Some PR GC 40, then PR GC 10 waymarking

**Equipment:** walking boots, sunhat, warm long trousers, long-sleeved shirt, warm fleece, warm jacket, gloves, raingear, picnic with high energy food, plenty of water

**Access:** 🚌 18 to Cruz Grande (Timetable 20; journey time 1h15min, including a 10-minute stop at San Bartolomé). Or 🚗: park at San Mateo and take 🚌 18 to Cruz Grande to start (journey time about 1h30min). Travelling from Las Palmas, take 🚌 303 (journey time 50min) or 🚗 to San Mateo, then change to 🚌 18 as above. *To return:* 🚌 18 from San Mateo to Maspalomas (Timetable 20; journey time about 2h45min) or 🚌 303 to Las Palmas (Timetable 9; journey time 50min). Or 🚗

**Short walk: Cruz Grande — Pico Nieves turn-off — Ayacata** (7km/4.5mi; 3h35min). Fairly strenuous (ascent of 500m/1600ft, descent of 450m/1500ft). Only suitable in fine weather. Equipment and access as above (🚗: park at Cruz Grande). Return: 🚌 18 (Timetable 20) from Ayacata — back to base, to Cruz Grande for your car, or to San Mateo to connect with 🚌 303 to Las Palmas. Leave the main walk at the 1h50min-point, where the ascent to Alto del Campanario begins. Instead of ascending, continue down the path for 15min, to the GC600. Turn left and follow this road to the parking area for Roque Nublo. Follow the Roque Nublo path for a few metres/yards, then fork left for Ayacata (PR GC 60), using the notes for Alternative walk 1 on page 41.

This hike begins on the magnificent old *camino real* that crosses the *cumbre* to the north. Concealed in the heights of this great barrier of rock lie two tiny vivid green reservoirs. Beyond these *presas* you tackle the toughest part of the walk — the ascent to the peaks: Alto del Campanario, with the best views on the island, and Pico de las Nieves, the highest point (1949m/6392ft). From these summits you descend the shoulders of the *cumbre*, winding down flower-covered slopes. A beautiful alpine valley, sprinkled with chestnut groves, leads you out into the island's fruitbowl, San Mateo.

**Start the walk** at the BUS STOP at **Cruz Grande**. Walk back through the pass towards San Bartolomé for 50m/yds, then ascend a concrete drive signposted 'PR GC 40, PICO DE LAS NIEVES/CAMINO DE SANTIAGO'. Pass to the right of a house and climb straight uphill; there are no turn-offs to worry about. You have a choice of views — the vast San Bartolomé basin to the east and, higher up, the shallow Ahogaderos Valley in the west. Tall agaves salute you on your way.

A CONCRETE MARKER (**25min**) is the first of many you will encounter (Picnic 12). Sheer rock walls soon tower above you, and the path can be seen twisting its way up the bulging mountainside ahead. Your view now stretches over the Ahogaderos Valley to the Embalse de Chira. A rock protruding from the mountain wall serves as a good LOOKOUT POINT (**40min**). Daisies splash bright white along your way. The path underfoot, shown overleaf, is a work of art, the island's masterpiece. Soon it winds its way up into the bulging mass of rock. A tiny green *presa* (reservoir) appears (**Charco Hondo**; **55min**), built into the rocky face of the escarpment below. With a sweeping panorama, this makes the ideal rest stop (another setting for Picnic 12; photograph pages 8-9).

After a zig and a zag above this contemplative spot, the cobbled trail ends. At first you will see nothing but bedrock, but look more closely — a worn path, marked by cairns, soon becomes obvious. It gradually bends over to the right and, 50m/yds uphill, passes between two rocks and follows a dry stream bed on the left, which it eventually crosses. San Bartolomé can be glimpsed through the pines, over the edge of the *cumbre*. Ignore a faint path to the right

(although it may be marked with a blue arrow; **1h30min**).

Just before the *camino real* heads downhill at the pass of **Degollada de los Hornos** (marked by an old sign, 'MONUMENTO NATURAL'; **1h50min**), you leave it to climb Alto del Campanario. *(But if you are doing the Short walk, or if bad weather threatens, remain on the main path.)* Pico de las Nieves houses a military installation and is accessible by road, hence no fun to climb. The peak just to the right of it, Alto del Campanario, is your target initially. In good weather this ascent is fairly easy and straightforward. A narrow, worn woodland path on the right, edged by small cairns, leads to the summit. After about five minutes' climb, the path goes left around the hillside, and a few minutes later it remounts the ridge. Take care at the pass of **Degollada de los Gatos** (**2h05min**), where the the main path bends left round the hillside: continue up the crest on a lesser path, keeping an eye out for the SMALL CAIRNS. Some eight minutes higher up, the path forks; both forks climb to the summit, but the left fork is preferable. Then bend right to ascend the rocky crown of **Alto del Campanario** (1926m/6317ft; **2h35min**). (The true summit, a rocky nodule, is a another two-minute scramble higher.) From here you can appreciate the vastness of the Caldera de Tirajana, the basin of San Bartolomé. The mountainside plummets hundreds of metres straight down into it. Keep away from this edge on windy or misty days! The wooded plain immediately below is Llanos de la Pez. This is the roof of the island.

To continue to Pico de las Nieves, retrace your steps down the rocky crown for a few minutes, keeping slightly left (over to the right the way is steep and awkward). Then go straight downhill. Three or four minutes later you arrive on the main contour path below the summit. Turn right on the contour path, pushing through

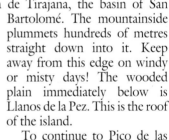

*View across the* cumbre *to Roque Nublo, with El Teide on Tenerife in the distance*

*Above and opposite: this old stone-laid* camino *across the* cumbre *is the island's masterpiece.*

broom and velvety-leafed *Lamiaceae* (ironwort). Ignore paths up to the right. After a good five minutes, the path joins the rim of the Caldera de Tirajana and, climbing steeply, stays on the rim or beside it all the way up to the roadside *mirador* at **Pico de las Nieves** (**3h10min**).

Follow the road downhill to a junction. The **Pozo de las Nieves**, a deep snow pit, is just to the right. Keep straight ahead on the GC135 for 'PICO DE LA GORRA', edging the *cumbre*. After two minutes, just before a HELIPAD on the left, turn left on a cobbled track which passes to the left of the 'POZO DE LA NIEVE GRANDE' (signposted). You descend into a narrow gully. Winding through scrub, stay in the gully. Passing through an abandoned, overgrown orchard, scramble down over stone walls. Chestnut trees abound. Joining a track, follow it to the right. Five minutes later, meet the GC130 (**3h40min**) and turn left.

After two minutes' ascent (about 150m/yds), take the first track to the right, into pines. Ignore a faint track to the right immediately and go straight ahead through an intersection. Ignore another track forking off to the right but, 100m/yds beyond it, fork right downhill on another *camino real* (a CAIRN marks this turn-off, but there may also be signposting for the PR GC 10). Back on the track again, follow it to the left downhill (ignoring a turn-off to the right). Some 100m/yds short of where the track ends, pick up the *camino real* again on the right, between stone walls. The hillside is a wild tangle of chestnut trees and

80

scrub, hiding an apple orchard.

Out of the scrub, step down
to the lone habitation of **Hoya
del Gamonal** (**4h15min**), a
pastoral outpost completely
encircled by hills. Follow the
track away from the home-
stead. After just two minutes
downhill, cut off a corner of
the track by descending a path
to the left into a cluster of
pines. Rejoin the track, turn
left and, after 20m/yds, take
the path left, descending the
hillside. Cross a small (dry)

stream and continue along its left bank, remaining on this
path until it drops down onto a track shaded by tall
eucalyptus trees. (A narrow strip of path along this stretch
may be unnerving for less experienced walkers.) Turn left
on a track, and follow this track for the next 15-20 minutes.

You leave this narrow verdant valley with a vista over
the northern hills, speckled with villages. A SQUARE
CONCRETE POST (**4h45min**) on the right-hand side of the
track marks the start of your next path. Cross a short
stretch of grassy hillside to a junction of tracks and take
the track straight ahead. San Mateo finally comes into view
below, squeezed in amongst the surrounding hills. After a
few minutes, where the track abruptly turns downhill to a
*barranco*, keep straight ahead on a path. Briefly skirting a
high fence to your left, climb a crest. Looking back into
this alpine valley from the crest, you catch it at its best.
Continuing on, the land immediately ahead is some of the
island's most productive.

Following the crest, descend to a ROAD (**5h15min**) and
follow it to the right for eight minutes (a good 700m/
0.4mi), ignoring all side-tracks. Then, when the road
bends sharply to the left, head uphill to the right on a track
along the slopes of **Montaña Troya**. It soon becomes a
path. Minutes later, descend a driveway down to another
road and follow this to the right. The road bends abruptly
downhill to the right, to the VALSEQUILLO ROAD (GC41),
where you turn left. Three minutes downhill, turn left
down a steep concrete lane (which recrosses the GC41
twice). A street takes you into **San Mateo**. On meeting
the main GC15, turn right to the BUS STATION, a few
minutes along, on your right (**5h55min**).

# Walk 13: LA CALDERILLA • TAIDIA • SANTA LUCIA

**Map begins on reverse of the touring map and ends on pages 88-89**

**Distance/time:** 8.5km/5.5mi; 3h25min

**Grade:** moderate, with an overall descent of 1000m/3300ft. You must b sure-footed and have a head for heights. Only suitable in fine weather. Ca be very cold and windy. PR GC 30 throughout

**Equipment:** walking boots, sunhat, long trousers, fleece, warm jacke gloves, rainwear, water, picnic

**Access and return:** 🚖 taxi from either San Mateo (via the GC600 an GC130), or Telde to a forestry track south of La Calderilla (or with friends This track turns south off the GC130 road 2.7km above the Caldera de la Marteles (coming from Telde), or 2.3km below the Los Pechos junctio (coming from San Mateo).
*To return:* 🚌 34 from Santa Lucía to Agüimes (Timetable 15; journey tim 30min), then 🚌 11 to Las Palmas (Timetable 14; journey time 45min).

**Shorter walk: Santa Lucía — Taídia — Santa Lucía** (5km/3mi; 2h15min Easy. Access: 🚖 or 🚌 to/from Santa Lucía (as above). Do the walk in reven (well signposted), contouring after an initial ascent of 150m/490ft. A goo option when the *cumbre* is in cloud; of course you *could* climb higher!

This walk is best kept for a fine day, when you'll hav striking views out over the Caldera de Tirajana. Walkin along the wall of the *cumbre*, all you'll hear is the shrill cry o the falcon. On the descent, palm-adorned villages hidden i side-valleys come out of hiding.

**Start the walk** on the FORESTRY TRACK just south of L

Calderilla. Ignore a turn-of left at the outset and stay o this track until it ends. Th summit of the *cumbre* i covered in *retama, codeso escobón* and pine groves. Soo you cross a plain sheltered b low rolling hills and plante with fruit trees. Ignore wide track to the righ (**25min**) and a turning to th left a few minutes late Several minutes later, a another turning to the left b the **Cruz del Socorro**, kee straight on; then ignore thre turn-offs to the right. Soo on the very edge of th escarpment — if the cloud are playing fair — you'll b rewarded with an exhilar ating view across the vas

*On the approach to Taídia*

asin of San Bartolomé, the most impressive on the island.

When you come to a T-junction, turn right. A couple of minutes later the TRACK ENDS (**55min**), and your path begins, running straight off the track. It is flanked by low stone walls at first. Admire the panorama before setting off. This convoluted path descends into a side-valley emptying out of the *cumbre*. The walls are covered in a mixture of bright green-leafed *tabaiba*, great specimens of *Aeonium, taginaste, verode, and sideritis*.

Santa Lucía, one of the island's prettiest villages, appears far below, set on an elevated shelf sprinkled with palms. The path descends a narrow ledge in the escarpment (unnerving for inexperienced walkers). Rounding the cliffs into the San Bartolomé valley, a view unfolds down to Taídia, spread across a hillside in this rugged corner of the *caldera*. The small town crammed on a hillside on the far side of the crater is San Bartolomé. Small lines of settlement trickle along the various valleys.

The path descends a ridge above the deep **Barranco Seco** on the right (**1h50min**). After 30 minutes, steps take you down to a CONCRETE LANE (**2h20min**) just above **Taídia**, a picturesque village flooded with palms and gardens. Cross the lane and descend the path/track opposite, into the gardens below. At the T-junction that follows, turn left. A minute later, at a fork, keep left between houses. Now keep straight ahead, ignoring all side-paths. Within five minutes, you rejoin the concrete lane. Follow it downhill to the right for 100m/yds, then take an earthen driveway to the left. Continue on the path leading left off the drive. Ignore a path to the right and, minutes later, join a track. Turn left and, after 100m/yds, turn right to take the path again.

Rounding the hillside, you pass through terraced plots lined with crumbled stone walls and grassy slopes. After a good 10 minutes on the path, ignore a turning to the left. Meet a FARM TRACK (**3h**), turn right and, after 20m/yds, rejoin the path. At the next track, again turn right and find the path after 20m/yds. A valley of palms opens up just below, and soon a you're looking down on Santa Lucía. After a few minutes you cross a minor track and descend along the edge of the valley above the village. Seven minutes below the minor track you'll find yourself in a trench. Follow it to the left downhill. Half a minute down, turn right down a gravelly, eroded path. When you come to a street, turn right to the church in **Santa Lucía** (**3h20min**). Take the steps opposite the church down to the main GC65. There are BUS STOPS left and right (**3h25min**).

## Walk 14: BANDAMA — PICO AND CALDERA

**Distance/time:** 9km/5.6mi; 3h45min

**Grade:** moderate, with an overall ascent/descent of 350m/1150ft. You mus
be sure-footed and have a head for heights: the descent into the crater is stee
and slippery; the detour to the caves and much of the path on the crater rir
is vertiginous (dangerous in wet and windy weather).

**Equipment:** walking boots, sunhat, long trousers, long-sleeved shirt, fleec
windproof, raingear, water, picnic

**Access and return:** 🚌 311 from Las Palmas to/from Bandama (Timetab
11; journey time 45min). Or 🚗: park in Bandama, off the side of the road

**Short walks:** The main walk can be divided into three parts, each of whic
makes a good short walk: **the peak**\* and its *mirador* (moderate, 180m/600
ascent/descent; 1h), **the crater floor** (fairly strenuous, 230m/750
descent/ascent; 1h30min), **the crater rim** (easy but vertiginous, 1h15min
Equipment and access/return as main walk.

U p to the peak, down into the crater and then round th
rim. You'll have seen Bandama from every possibl
angle when you've done this walk. Guanche caves, se
spectacularly in the sheer walls of this perfectly-formed crater
make an intriguing detour.

**Start the walk** in **Bandama**, at the JUNCTION of th
GC802 to La Atalaya and the GC822 to Pico de Bandam
(20m/yds uphill from the bus stop). Just follow the roa
signposted PICO DE BANDAMA\*, rising above dark shallow
valleys that nurture some of the island's few vineyards. (A
the end of the walk you might like to visit the Bodega Sa
Juan de Mocanal, a few minutes' drive away on the GC802
This large old property, with a wine museum, is set in a park.
At the top of **Pico de Bandama** (**35min**), you'll find a ba
and coachloads of tourists. Wonderful views encircle yo
here. Ridges stream down off the *cumbre*. Las Palmas, alway
at its best when seen from a distance, is a sprawl of whit
stretching all the way along to the prominent Isleta. And th
crater lies below, 200m/650ft deep, 1000m/3300ft i
diameter.

To explore the floor of the crater, walk back down the roa
to the junction and go on to the BUS STOP on the La Atalay
road (**1h**). From the bus stop, go left on a driveway (signpost
'CALDERA DE BANDAMA'), into the tight cluster of houses. Jus
beyond a gate, you pass a *mirador* overlooking the *caldero*
(Note the sign on the gate saying that it is only open betwee
08.00 and 17.00; bear this in mind for your return from th
crater floor.) High stone walls flank your cobbled path; i
quickly falls away into the crater, where the walls are covere
in a wild tangle of prickly pear, lavender and *vinagrera*.

\*There used to be a path to the summit (shown with dots on our map), bu
it has become overgrown with spiky agaves. Obviously, if you are in a ca
you may prefer to drive the first part of this walk.

Approaching the first bend, where the (now-earthen) path
rns sharp right, you can take a detour to visit the Guanche
ves (timings included in the main walk). Take a path
cending slightly to the left. This narrow gravelly path
osses a steep slope and inexperienced walkers may find it
nerving. Some eight minutes across the wall of the crater,
)u come to the MAIN GUANCHE CAVES (**1h15min**), set high
the escarpment.

From these caves return to the main path. Just after join-
g it, you come to another *mirador* built onto a rocky

*e Casas del Fondo in the Caldera de Bandama*

outcrop. Don't lean on the railings here! About 10 minutes below the *mirador,* as you approach the floor of the crater (just past an enormous boulder on the right; **1h35min**), turn right to circle the crater. At a fork encountered immediately, keep left. Your path heads round the lower crater walls amidst a scattering of olive trees. After five minutes, a path joins from the right. The crater shelters an interesting mixture of vegetation — palms, eucalyptus, *retama, taginaste,* olive trees, and higher up, *cardón.*

Soon you reach an *era* (circular threshing floor). Remain on the path to the right here, heading towards the very picturesque ruined farm buildings and garden plots in the crater floor, **Casas del Fondo** (**1h55min**). Pass below the gardens, ignoring the path off right that runs alongside the house. Keep an eye out for an old wine press behind the farm sheds. Two enormous eucalyptus trees offer shade here, and there's also a water tap.

From the water tap continue to the main path and turn right, back to the JUNCTION ABOVE THE BUS STOP (**2h30min**). Turn right and follow the Pico de Bandama road. All the way round, you're looking straight down into the crater. After six minutes, where the road bends almost 90° to the left, turn sharp right down a path. After five minutes' descent, you will reach the edge of the crater and mount the crest. A path appears, running inside the rim. This spectacular ramble round the perimeter is just at the crater's edge and quite vertiginous. There are fine views off the shoulder of the crater over villages sheltering amongst the surrounding hills.

Within an hour of circling the crater (just below a hotel and golf course), the path suddenly turns left to climb to a corner of the green. Keeping along the edge of the green, head across to the hotel; walk through the car park and take the gravel track out. At a fork, keep to the chained-off, lower track, above the tennis courts. Just after rejoining the golf course road, you meet the Atalaya road (GC802). Follow it to the right downhill, back to the BUS STOP and bar (**3h45min**).

86

## Walk 15: SAN BARTOLOME • CRUZ GRANDE • DEGOLLADA DE LA MANZANILLA • SAN BARTOLOME

**Distance/time:** 13km/8mi; 4h15min

**Grade:** moderate; fairly steep ascent of 350m/1150ft and gradual descent. *Highly recommended* for reasonably fit beginners, but not in wet weather. PR CG 40 throughout

**Equipment:** walking boots, sunhat, long trousers, long-sleeved shirt, warm fleece, windproof, picnic, plenty of water

**Access and return:** 🚗 to/from San Bartolomé. Or 🚌 18 (Timetable 20) to/from San Bartolomé; journey time 50min. From Las Palmas take 🚌 11 to Agüimes (Timetable 14; journey time 45min), then change to 🚌 34 to San Bartolomé (Timetable 15; journey time 50min); use the same buses to return, or else take 🚌 18 to Faro de Maspalomas (Timetable 20), then 🚌 30 to Las Palmas (Timetable 19).

If clouds threaten bad weather in the north, head south to walk. Although the devastating fires of summer 2007 have left their traces in this area, there is still much of beauty to accompany you along the *camino real*.

**The walk starts** on the west side of the GC60 in **San Bartolomé**, 65m/yds north of the BUS STOP and about an equal distance south of the church. Ascend CALLE PADRE CLARET (opposite Calle Pérez Galdós), climbing steeply. At the top, turn left on CALLE CORAZON DE JESUS and remain on this street (later called CALLE DE SAN JUAN) until you pass below the CEMETERY and come to a junction opposite a SCHOOL. Walk just a few metres to the left, then turn right on CALLE JUGLAR FABIAN TORRES, running just to the left of the school. After three minutes, just past two rows of houses on the right (**20min**), turn right on a track signposted 'CAMINO REAL, CRUZ GRANDE, CUMBRE' (there may also be a PR GC 40 sign).

After couple of minutes, when the track bends left, continue straight ahead on the *camino real,* in a landscape full of *Cistus, tabaiba, retama,* aloes, *taginaste, Salvia blanca* and *escobón*. A fine cobbled trail comes underfoot, climbing to the upper reaches of the **Barranco de Tirajana**. Eventually you join a track (**1h20min**): turn left uphill to **Cruz Grande**, a signposted pass on the GC60.

Follow this road to the left and, after 40m/yds (just through the pass), turn left on a forestry track (initially concreted). This track will remain your way for the next 1h45min, as far as the Degollada de la Manzanilla. Ignore two tracks to the right (the second goes to a *casa forestal*). Your view reaches out over the wooded valley of the Barranco de los Ahogaderos. And behind you the *cumbre* rears up, an imposing mass of rock. Some 25 minutes from the road, when the track swings sharp left, ignore a path

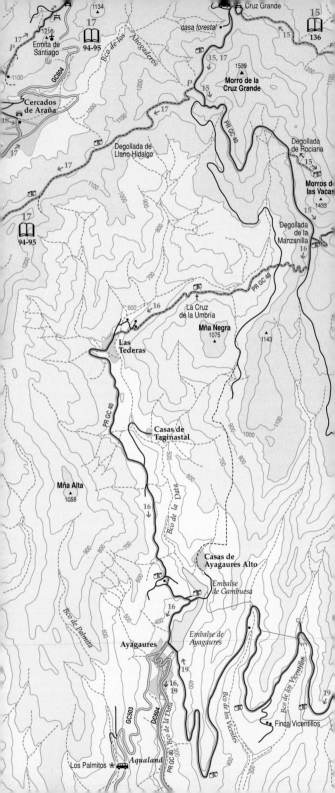

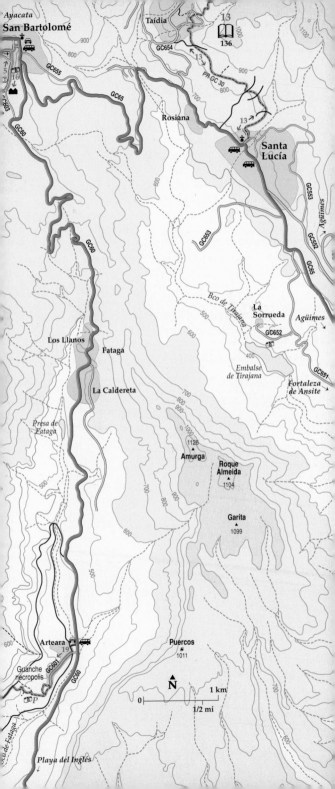

to the right (the route of Walk 17). You look out over the enormous **Barranco de la Data** here (Picnic 15). Soon, ignore a track to the right.

About 1h20min from the road (just after rounding a slight bend; **2h45min**), you could make an optional 12-minute return detour to the Degollada de Rociana, a fine viewpoint over the extensive Barranco de Tirajana and San Bartolomé: keep an eye out for a wide path ascending to the left, by a small CAIRN.

When you reach the pass (**Degollada de la Manzanilla; 3h10min**), take the first track to the left, for San Bartolomé. The pass affords a fine view over the upper Fataga Valley. Descending, the way narrows into a path and soon rubs against the hillside, where high craggy fingers of rock pierce the ridge above. Widening into a track again, your route eventually goes straight through an INTERSECTION (**3h50min**). Beyond some piggeries, you join a road coming from the right and follow it to the left, ignoring a wide track off to the left. Five minutes later, fork right to a road (ANTONIO SANTANA). Turn left, passing the STADIUM on your left, and a few minutes later keep right, to descend back to **San Bartolomé (4h15min)**.

*View over the route descending from the Degollada de la Manzanilla to San Bartolomé, with the Barranco de Fataga in the distance*

## Walk 16: SAN BARTOLOME • DEGOLLADA DE LA MANZANILLA • LAS TEDERAS • AYAGAURES • (AQUALAND)

See map pages 88-89; see also photograph page 12 and opposite

**Distance/time:** 13.5km/8.3mi; 4h30min *or* 22.5km/14mi; 6h30min if you follow PR GC 40 all the way to Aqualand.

**Grade:** easy-moderate, but quite long, with an overall descent of 950m/3100ft (1150m/3800ft if you go all the way to Aqualand). Unsuitable in wet weather. PR GC 40 waymarking throughout

**Equipment:** walking boots, sunhat, long trousers, long-sleeved shirt, warm fleece, windproof, raingear, picnic, plenty of water

**Access:** 🚍 to San Bartolomé, as Walk 15, page 87. 🚗 Motorists should park at Maspalomas/Playa del Inglés, then take the bus to start.
*To return:* 🚕 taxi from Ayagaures to Playa del Inglés (best arranged in advance, together with a meeting point by the dam). Or, if you walk on to Aqualand, 🚍 45 from there to Playa del Inglés (Timetable 21; journey time 6min. Change to 🚍 30 for Las Palmas (Timetable 19; journey time 1h10min).

Señor Pedro, a local farmer, was the highlight of this hike on my first visit, many years ago. Both of us were on our way down into the Barranco de la Data, a massive elongated canyon, he to work, me to stroll. He took me under his wing, pointing out places of interest. He loved his valley, sad that no tourists ever ventured this far, and hoped, to my horror, that one day a road would be built here. This still hasn't happened, and the only communication with the outside world is still the 6km-long rough track followed in this walk. Las Tederas, the remote hamlet Señor Pedro told me about, was just as peaceful as he claimed ... and as beautiful.

**The walk starts** on the GC60 in **San Bartolomé**, 65m/ yds uphill from (north of) the bus stop. Ascend CALLE PADRE CLARET on the left, climbing steeply through the village. At the top of the street, turn left on CALLE CORAZON DE JESUS. Then ignore two streets to the left. At the T-junction, turn left on CALLE SAN JUAN, then turn left again up CALLE EL ROQUE. Above the town, at a junction, turn left. From a roadside lookout, there's a good view over the enormous segmented Barranco de Tirajana. Santa Lucía (Walk 13) sits across the valley to the east. The whitish fragmented hillock protruding out of the far valley wall is Risco Blanco.

After a few minutes along the road, just beyond the Hotel Las Tirajanas and the *campo de futból*, turn right (sign: 'DEGOLLADA DE MANZANILLA'; 'PR GC 40'). At the T-junction that follows, turn left. After two minutes keep left at a fork with a track. Almond trees dot the lower slopes, pines the upper slopes. You are making for the range of high hills ahead. At the fork that follows, keep right for 'DEGOLLADA DE MANZANILLA'. Follow this past some smelly PIGGERIES (**45min**). About 15 minutes later, if you encounter a small rockfall, cross it with care.

A steady ascent takes you up to a pass, the **Degollada de la Manzanilla** (**1h15min**), from where you enjoy a superb view over both the immense Barranco de la Data in the south, and the upper reaches of the Barranco de Fataga. Turn left at the pass ('MASPALOMAS' sign), down into the **Barranco de la Data**; there's no sign of life in this completely enclosed valley. After 10 minutes, take the cobbled path descending to the right. Pink-flowering rock roses *(Cistus)* cover the otherwise bare stony slopes. You cross a forestry track and continue descending below Montaña Negra. A famous, massive 400 year old pine tree used to rise on this path; it was damaged by the fires of July 2007 (the worst ecological disaster ever seen on the island) and felled by high winds in January 2008. No doubt a plaque will eventually mark its passing.

Continue straight ahead from here, passing **La Cruz de Umbría** (**2h55min**). This square lump of rock with a concrete cross and a plaque reading 'DESCANSADEROS DE LOS MUERTES', marks the place where people from Ayagaures rested when carrying their dead over the mountains for burial near San Bartolomé. Rounding a bend in the escarpment, **Las Tederas** gradually comes out of hiding. This drawn-out string of typical country dwellings, some dating back 200 years, is only used as a weekend retreat, when the villagers return to tend their plots. Palm trees grace the valley floor, although Las Tederas was particularly badly affected by the fires of 2007. Your path is now an old cobbled trail. Not far downhill you pass above some garden plots. The path leads past an old building and then immediately drops to the right, to a TRACK (**2h40min**). What appears to be the main village homestead lies along to the right. But turn *left* here and, after a short distance, you will rejoin your path on the left. Disappearing into scrub, it takes you down to the valley floor, where you cross the stream bed and pick up the path again, climbing left up to a track.

Before continuing, look back up the valley you've just descended and to Las Tederas in its splendid setting. Then turn left along the track, which you will follow all the way to Ayagaures. Impressive ridges rise on both sides of the valley. After 40 minutes on the track (**3h30min**), ignore a track turning off to the left and, a few minutes later, a minor track to the right. Soon the picturesque Embalse de Gambuesa appears unexpectedly, set deep in the valley. Then the hamlet of Casas de Ayagaures Alto, just a smattering of houses, reveals itself in its prize position overlooking the dam. From a PASS (**4h**), another mud-green dam, the Embalse de Ayagaures, comes into view below. You can take a short-cut here: go left, then turn right downhill just past a small building. An path then takes you back down to the main track. Seven minutes further down the track, take the second turning left, towards Casas de Ayagaures Alto. This three minute detour leads to the edge of the **Embalse de Gambuesa**, a vast reservoir by Canarian standards, backed by the palm-adorned village. It's a beauty spot few tourists see; don't miss it!

Back on the main track, continue to the left, to **Ayagaures** (**4h30min**), once a small farming community, but now boasting some fancy homes. *(Walk 19 joins here, from the left.)* Pick up your pre-arranged taxi on the far side of the dam wall. Or, if you're still full of bounce, follow the PR GC 40 waymarks and continue down the road (GC 504) through the small village and then through the Barranco de la Data for another two hours, until you reach the road to Los Palmitos Park to the right and Maspalomas to the left. Pick up Bus 45 (the Los Palmitos bus) at AQUALAND, remembering that the last bus leaves just after 18.00.

*Las Tederas — before the devastating fires of 2007*

# Walk 17: CRUZ GRANDE • EMBALSE DE CHIRA • MONTAÑA DE SANTIAGO • GC60

Map begins on pages 88-89, ends below; see also photo page 98-99

**Distance/time:** 13.5km/8.5mi; 4h30min

**Grade:** moderate; descent of 300m/1000ft and ascent of 200m/660ft. You must be sure-footed and have a head for heights. Not suitable in wet weather, when the rocky hillsides are dangerously slippery.

**Equipment:** walking boots, sunhat, long trousers, long-sleeved shirt, warm fleece, windproof, raingear, picnic, plenty of water

**Access:** 🚌 to Cruz Grande: see Walk 12, page 77. 🚗 Motorists could park near Cruz Grande and walk (or take a bus) back to their cars (3km). *To return:* 🚌 18 to San Bartolomé; catch it at the turn-off to the Embalse de Chira on the GC60 (Timetable 20; departs a few minutes after leaving Ayacata; journey time 20min). See Walk 15, page 87, for return 🚌 from San Bartolomé if you are continuing to Las Palmas.

Starting on a popular hiking trail, this walk descends to the Embalse de Chira, an impressive reservoir. It then visits the charming rustic village of Cercados de Araña, near the tail of the reservoir. And the finale of the hike takes in one of the island's little known gems, an overgrown ravine, hemmed in by two enormous loaves of rock, with small cave-dwellings hidden in the tangle of vegetation.

**Cruz Grande** is just a signposted pass on the ridge between two vast valleys, the Barranco de Tirajana and the Barranco de los Ahogaderos. From the BUS STOP, **start out** by walking back the way the bus came, following the GC60 towards San Bartolomé. Just before the pass, turn right on a forestry track (initially concreted; also the route of Walk 15, the PR GC 40). Ignore two tracks to the right (the second goes to a *casa forestal*). Stay on this forestry track until it curves sharp left (**25min**). Here, descend a path to the right, down into the enormous **Barranco de la Data**. The steep winding path leads you along the dry stony ridge dividing the Data and Ahogaderos valleys. Ignore all paths off left, down into the *barranco*. Your route crosses to the right-hand side of the ridge (**1h05min**). After 20 minutes, ignore a fork to the left. From the top of the ridge there is a superb view over the lake-sized Embalse de Chira and the village of Cercados de Araña.

After another 20 minutes (**1h45min**), leave this path: now referring to the map opposite, turn right on a steep gravel path

94

*Looking back along the first rock 'loaf' (3h 35min en route)*

which twists down to a forestry track. Descend the track for a couple of minutes. When you see an enclosed water tank below, go behind it to find two water pipes aiming straight for the dam. Follow the minor path alongside them. A few minutes down, you'll find it easier to cross the pipes and keep to the left of them. You cross a ditch on a bridge (the handrails of the bridge are visible before you reach it) just before meeting the road at the **Embalse de Chira (2h15min)**.

Turn right on the road. After 30 minutes, just as you enter **Cercados de Araña (2h45min)**, turn left at a junction (by a sign 'CENTRO URBANO'). Keep straight on for a couple of minutes, ignoring turn-offs to the left. At a parking area with a bar/restaurant (closed/for sale at time of writing) on the right, turn left on a track, passing house (N° 27, CASA MEIJAS. The track runs through orchards and vegetable plots set along the valley floor. Crossing a small

bridge, and ignoring all side tracks, rise to a rough gravel road. From here you look across a tiny inlet of water to the little houses of Cercados de Araña, peering out of prickly pear cacti (photograph overleaf).

Turn left on the road. Go left at the first two T-junctions but, at the third T-junction (some 600m/yds from the bridge, at the brow of the hill), turn right. Beyond an ENCLOSED FIELD OF PRICKLY PEAR, go through a chain barrier and continue on a minor track. Some 70m/yds further on, turn right at a fork. Follow this narrow track gently uphill. Behind you, the upper walls of the Soria Valley appear in the south. Some 125m/yds along, above a small DAM, turn left on a faint path, skirting to the left of the dam and another, smaller dam just beyond it. This path takes you to a larger reservoir, the **Presa de Bernadino**.

Cross the dam wall, then (beyond a fine VIEWPOINT) continue up the crest for five minutes, until you are below a first rock 'loaf'. Here you should find a water channel cut into the hillside. Turn right along it; a path will soon appear. Enjoy the panorama back over the Chira reservoir and Cercados de Araña.

The path runs by the foot of the rock loaf. After a few minutes, you come to a stream bed. Cross it and, a minute later, keep left at a fork. Passing a first CAVE HOUSE (N° 14; **3h35min**), round the hillside into a tiny hidden ravine, the highlight of this hike (Picnic 17). Descending to the stream bed, you're caught up in a tangle of prickly pear, aloes, almond and fig trees that fill the ravine floor.

Your general direction is up the valley floor, but little paths turn off here and there which are great fun to explore! You'll find fascinating cave-dwellings in every corner, most of them in decay. *(Watch out for broken glass.)* It takes about takes about 10 minutes to pass through this jungle of vegetation, then you ascend a path through a strip of terracing at the left. This takes you to a track, and a handful of houses snuggled into the hillside. Climb the track, but don't forget the views behind!

After 15 minutes you come to the **Zona Recreativa Montaña de Santiago** (**4h05min**). Ignoring a track to the left, follow the track out of the picnic area to the Embalse de Chira road. Turn left for 15 minutes, to the GC60 (**4h30min**), where you can flag down the bus. Or, if no bus is due for a while, you could turn left towards Ayacata and walk 1km to Bar Candelilla. Have some refreshments and wait for a bus there.

# Walk 18: DEGOLLADA DEL ASERRADOR • CRUCE DE LA DATA • SORIA • CERCADOS DE ARAÑA

Map begins on the reverse of the touring map and ends on pages 94-95; see also photograph page 104

**Distance/time:** 16.5km/10mi; 5h50min

**Grade:** very strenuous, with an overall descent of 700m/2300ft and ascent of 300m/1000ft. You must be sure-footed and have a head for heights. Only suitable in fine weather; the walk can be cold and windy.

**Equipment:** walking boots, sunhat, fleece, windproof, long trousers, rainwear, picnic, plenty of water

**Access:** 🚌 or 🚐 18 (Timetable 20) to the Degollada del Aserrador; journey time about 2h.
*To return:* 🚌 pre-arranged taxi from Cercados de Araña (point our the exact place on the map!) or telephone when you get there. *Or* follow Walk 17 from the 2h45min-point to the GC60 for a bus — back to base, or back to your car (add 1h45min).

**Short walk: Soria — Cruce de la Data — Soria** (6km/3.7mi; 2h 40min). Moderate, with an ascent of 260m/850ft. Otherwise grade and equipment as above. Access by 🚌 car to the end of the tarred road beyond Soria (ample parking). Follow the continuing track gently uphill to Cruce de la Data, then pick up the main walk at the 2h20min-point. When you meet the tarred road at Soria, follow it left, back to your car. *Highly recommended,* but the lovely waterfall en route may be dry in summer.

F ew tourists venture off the beaten track into the rugged interior of the island. It's dramatic and strikingly beautiful in its grandeur, but it will cost you dearly in energy. If you're fit, don't miss it!

**Start out** on the GC60 at the **Degollada del Aserrador**. Walk along the road signposted to 'EL JUNCAL'. As you approach a bend to the left (opposite a crash barrier; **10min**), climb a path to the left up the scrub-covered hillside. On reaching the top of the crest, turn right along it. Already the scenery is superb. Ridges rise into imposing walls of rock; the Barranco de Ayacata slides away to the left, Barranco del Juncal to the right. The village strung out along the far wall of the valley on the right is El Juncal.

This clear path winds its way along the crest; there are no turn-offs. Massive valleys slice through the interior of the island. Wooded hillsides and the reservoirs of Chira and Cueva de las Niñas enhance the already-spellbinding scenery. You meet a FORESTRY TRACK at a 'crossroads' (**Cruz de la Huesita; 1h50min**). Leave the track immediately: turn left on a path which descends the side of the ridge. *(But for Walk 20, continue along the forestry track.)*

Drop down to the GC605 at KM64.7 (**Cruce de la Data; 2h20min**; *the Short walk joins here*). Cross the road and set off on the narrow tarmac road (closed to motor traffic by a barrier) going towards the dam wall. Almost immediately, turn left on a gravel track; there are farm buildings to your left, and this track *may be* signposted to 'SORIA'. Leave this track after 200m/yds (when the track swings sharp left): turn right on a path, heading round the edge of the high basin that cradles the **Embalse de la Cueva de las Niñas**. After five minutes, you cross a steep rocky face. Your continuing path lies a short way down the hillside. Briefly rejoining the ROAD TO THE DAM WALL (**2h35min**), turn left. After 250m/yds (at another sign, 'SORIA 1500m'), pick up the path again as it ascends to the left. Keep on the side of the ridge, below the crest, now referring to the map on pages 94-95.

Soon the isolated village of Soria appears, set high on the walls of the valley below, spreading across a cultivated hillside with a wonderful outlook over the island's deepest dam. The descent is breathtaking. Soon you come to one of my (many) favourite spots: a rocky *barranco* cut into the side of the ridge, with a waterfall and several small reed-filled pools in the floor (**3h15min**). Below, another high cascade drops into the valley. *Keep away from the edge!*

The route continues across the stream bed, and then edges its way round the steep hillside. (Some people will find this short stretch vertiginous.) A few minutes later, you join a track and follow it down to a road (**3h25min**).

For a 15-minute return detour to a superbly-sited deserted village (not included in the timings), turn left along the road, then turn right following the signs for 'Víveres Sara'. After a minute, just before Víveres Sara (an interesting place to refuel), keep right on a path that passes to the right of this bar/shop. Go left at the fork  two minutes later, to come to the village (Picnic 18b), beauti-

fully perched on a rocky outcrop just above the dam.

The main walk turns *right* on the road. After 10 minutes you reach a village shop and a restaurant in **Soria**. Turn left downhill past the restaurant, to make for the awesome wall of the **Embalse de Soria (3h40min)**, built across a very deep, narrow defile. Climb the steps at the far end of the dam wall, to the overflow, then turn left and follow the concrete path alongside it (Picnic 18a). After just 15m/yds along the path, above a couple of stone buildings, turn left. A formidable wall of rocky protrusions lies ahead. The route heads up the V of a small valley.

Some 20 minutes from the dam wall, ignore a minor path joining from the right. Ascending rapidly, you have a fine view over the **Barranco de Arguineguín**. Now high in the rocky upper reaches of the valley, scramble over bedrock, where the path becomes a little vague. Keep ascending to the left, following traces of the old path. When you reach a gentle valley hidden amidst all this rock, cross a TRACK (**4h35min**) and ascend the left side of the valley. Again, the rocky surface makes this somewhat vertiginous path difficult to follow. A couple of minutes after crossing a minor track, you join another track. Follow it to the right uphill. The pretty hamlet on the opposite ridge is Lomo de la Palma. Passing through a chain barrier, you come to a JUNCTION (**4h50min**): turn left.

Mounting the crest, the Embalse de Chira comes into sight, with your final destination, Cercados de Araña, sprawled around its tail. You cross a rocky plateau, where the *cumbre* rises boldly out of the landscape ahead. Ignore a turning left but, eight minutes later, take a short-cut to the left, following a line of telephone poles. A few minutes later, cross the track and continue on the path. When small CAIRNS lead you back to the track, turn right along it, and ignore a track to the left. Little white houses sit like ornaments all around the **Embalse de Chira**.

At a FORK (**5h35min**) keep right; the 'no entry' sign here is for vehicles only. After three minutes, you pass through a staggered junction, and then keep right at a fork. Beyond a stream you come to a parking area. Turn right off it and keep straight ahead to join the dam road at **Cercados de Araña (5h50min)**, by a TELEPHONE KIOSK. Your taxi should be waiting here, or you can phone one.

*Cercados de Araña and the Embalse de Chira (Walks 17 and 18)*

## Walk 19: ARTEARA • GUANCHE CEMETERY • AYAGAURES • LOS PALMITOS

See map pages 88-89; see also photographs pages 12, 32

**Distance/time:** 13km/8mi; 3h50min *or* 22km/13.6mi; 5h50min if you go all the way to Aqualand

**Grade:** quite easy (mostly along a contouring track)

**Equipment:** walking shoes, sunhat, long-sleeved shirt, windproof, rainwear, picnic, plenty of water

**Access:** 🚌 18 to Arteara (Timetable 20; journey time 25min). Or 🚌 30 from Las Palmas to Faro de Maspalomas (Timetable 19; journey time 1h15min), then 🚌 18. By 🚗: park at Maspalomas and take 🚌 18. *To return:* as Walk 16, page 91

**Shorter walk: Arteara — Guanche cemetery — Barranco de los Vicentillos — Arteara** (9km/5.5mi; 2h30min). Easy, mostly along a contouring track. Equipment, access as main walk, or 🚗: park in Arteara's large parking area, near the bus stop. Follow the main walk to the 1h15min-point and return the same way.

The highlight of this hike is the Guanche cemetery — a mass of simple stone graves, lost to the unobservant eye, in a vast welter of rock — an enormous centuries-old landslide. And this blemish in an emerald green, palm-laden valley floor comes up just at the outset of the walk. Then you move on into dry and desolate wasteland. In solitude you'll wind in and out of *barrancos,* hemmed in by high craggy ridges. On this easily-followed track, you can put yourself into top gear and roll along.

The bus drops you just at the edge of the **Barranco de Fataga**, opposite the small settlement of Arteara. **Start the walk** from the large village car park *(aparcamiento):* join the village road and walk through **Arteara**. All along the road you're peering into a breathtaking tangle of colour on your left: vegetables, corn, citrus and fig trees, tropical fruits, grape vines, purple-flowering sage, geraniums, flowering cacti, needle-leafed *valo,* mountain sage, palms and bougainvillea.

When the road ends (**15min**), steps lead up to the 'PARQUE ARQUEOLOGICO DE ARTEARA' visitors' centre. Even if it's closed, you can follow marked trails with information boards through the river of strewn rock shown on page 32. This huge GUANCHE NECROPOLIS is one of the island's most impressive ruins. Dozens and dozens of tombs lie amidst this debris of rock, but they lay unprotected for centuries (when I first came here in the 1980s, the remains of bones were scattered about).

Take ROUTE B, which ends at a wooden viewpoint overlooking the valley. (You might like to take the path circling back to Arteara on the return if you are doing the Shorter walk.) Past this *mirador* (Picnic 19) be sure to

*Cardón (cande-labra spurge)*

follow the CAIRN-MARKED PATH up the hill — at first rising gently, then quite steeply. On reaching a TRACK (**30min**), turn left (*note the* CAIRN *here for your return,* if you are doing the Shorter walk). This gravel track will take you west to Ayagaures. Ignore all side tracks; the only place where you may be in doubt is soon after joining the track, where you must keep right, slightly uphill (this junction is shown on the map, at the bottom of the left-hand page).

A high craggy wall marks your departure from the Fataga Valley; later you swing into one of its little tributaries (**1h**), full of greenery. Great fractured ridges block out the early-morning sun, and all you can see is ridge upon ridge upon ridge, lined and severe. Great clumps of candelabra spurge flourish below the track.

The track takes you into a third *barranco*, the **Barranco de los Vicentillos** (**1h15min**) — don't miss the delightful shaded cascade and pool a minute up the track at the apex of this *barranco*. (*The Shorter walk turns back here.*) Ignore a turning left down to the Finca Vicentillos. Five minutes later you round the nose of a ridge and come upon the **Barranco de los Vicentes** (**1h55min**) stretching straight back into the hills, occupied by one small house and a large citrus orchard. Beyond the house you overlook a garden stretching along the valley floor. A gap in the distant ravine reveals the sands of Maspalomas. A tinge of tired yellow sweeps across the landscape, but purple-flowering Canary sage is the most memorable feature of this hike. In winter the inclines are vivid green with *tabaiba*.

Crossing the final ridge, the **Barranco de la Data** tumbles away before you (**3h10min**; photograph page 12). In contrast to the ravines just passed, there is settlement here, and the valley floor is alive with cultivation. in a couple of minutes the village of Ayagaures and its reservoir reveal themselves. Cross the wall of the **Embalse de Ayagaures** (**3h50min**) and meet your pre-arranged taxi on the far side, in **Ayagaures**. Or join the road and turn left. Walk 16 comes in here from the track on the right: use the notes on page 93 to follow the PR GC 40 down the GC 504 to AQUALAND (5h50min).

## Walk 20: DEGOLLADA DEL ASERRADOR • EMBALSE DE LA CUEVA DE LAS NIÑAS • MONTAÑA DE TAURO • LAS CASILLAS

Map begins on reverse of the touring map and ends opposite

Distance/time: 21.5km/13.5mi; 7h10min

Grade: strenuous and long, with an overall descent of 1100m/3600ft, some of it very steep, and an ascent of 200m/660ft. You must be sure-footed and have a head for heights. Not suitable in bad weather, as there are *no* villages on route where you could shelter or telephone for a taxi.

Equipment: walking boots, sunhat, fleece, windproof, long trousers, picnic and extra snacks, *plenty of water*

Access: 🚌 18 (Timetable 20) to the Degollada del Aserrador; journey time about 2h.
*To return:* 🚌 38 from Las Casillas to Puerto de Mogán (Timetable 18; journey time 20min), then 🚌 to Playa del Inglés (🚌 32; Timetable 23 or 🚌 01; Timetable 22); journey time 50min. Or 🚌 01 to Las Palmas (Timetable 22; journey time 1h45min).

Alternative walk: Degollada del Asserador — Embalse Cueva de las Niñas — Degollada del Asserador (20km/12.4mi; 6h45min). Stren-uous and long, with a descent and ascent of 450m/1475ft. Equipment and access as main walk, or 🚗: park at the Degollada del Asserador. Follow the main walk via the Cruz de la Huesita to the GC605, then turn *left*. From Cruce de la Data, follow Walk 18 (in reverse) back to Cruz de la Huesita , then retrace your outgoing route up to the Asserador Pass.

T his has got to be the mother of all hikes! Traipsing across the uninhabited centre of the island, you soak up views in all directions: reservoirs as big as lakes, enor-mous sunken valleys, and rocky plateaus. The only other sign of human life out here will be a shepherd or two, if you're lucky, and maybe the odd hiker. It's blissfully quiet.

**Start out by** following Walk 18 (page 97) to the **Cruz de la Huesita** (**1h50min**), where Walk 18 turns left on a path. Continue along the forestry track until you reach the GC605 (**2h55min**), where you turn right to follow the road. *(The Alternative walk turns left on the road here.)* Ignore the gravel road heading north from the **Cruz de San Antonio**; keep to the road. From the narrow crest of the ridge there's a striking view along the length of **Embalse de la Cueva de las Niñas** to the left; to the right the idyllic green Embalse del Mulato lies deep in a wooded valley. The *barranco*s of Mogán and Veneguera supply the impressive backdrop.

A couple of minutes beyond the viewpoint turn left on a track signposted 'Finca Cortijo Majada Alta' (**3h 20min**). Now referring to the map opposite, go round the large gate here and follow the track downhill through rocky terrain flecked with luminous green *tabaiba*. After 10 minutes you pass through the remains of a second gateway. Five minutes later, turn right at a fork.

102

Small flocks of sheep graze amidst the rock-smeared inclines, and you continue past a pastoral outpost consisting of a couple of corrals (**3h40min**). Down in the valley, not far ahead, a couple of buildings snuggle into the crest of the ridge. However, don't go that far: at a turning/parking area (just before the track crosses a small stream), turn right on a faint path alongside the stream. Small cairns and the odd strip of low stone wall are your guides. After a few minutes, just over another stream, turn left to cross the stream you followed from the parking area. *Keep an eye on the cairns.*

Surmounting a crest, a gigantic rock with eye-shaped caves in it catches your attention. Over the crest, follow the clear path, heading right (again watching for strips of low stone wall). The path passes below and to the left of the 'eye-rock' and, five minutes later, dips down to a track beside a tiny dam, the **Presa del Salto del Perro**. Climb the track out of the *barranco,* up to the EL BARRANQUILLO DE SAN ANDRES ROAD (**4h10min**). Turn left and, after some 100m/yds, turn right up a stone-paved ramp. The walk now climbs towards the high barrier of hills to the left. A flat-topped crest

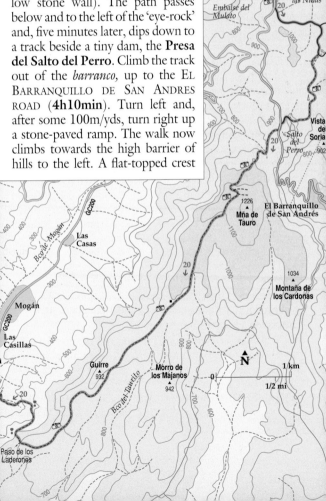

reached 15 minutes above the road offers fine views towards the nature reserve of Ojeda, Inagua and Pajonales, visited in Walk 21.

A steep ascent follows, into pine woodland. Climbing past two turnings to the left, two minutes apart, you arrive at a level shoulder of ridge (**4h45min**) below **Montaña de Tauro**. A spectacular landscape unfolds below: the top of the ridge flattens out into a long tongue of land stretching to the coast, covered by *Cistus*. In the distance to the left lie the dunes of Maspalomas. The route is straightforward from here on: just follow the path; it gradually bends to the right, with gaping valleys falling away on either side.

After contouring for a little over 30 minutes, you pass the remains of a STONE BUILDING near the edge of the cliff, which offers a bird's eye view over Mogán (**5h20min**). Sharp severe ridges cut across the northwestern corner of the island. Keep an eye out along this stretch for the quite rare *cardoncillo*, with finger-shaped stems; it grows just beside the path. From time to time the path returns to the edge of the plateau high above the Barranco de Mogán, with its tapestry of gardens and orchards.

The real descent begins at the **Paso de los Laderones** (**6h15min**). Ignore a minor path to the left and take the breathtaking path built into the cliff-face, down into the **Barranco de Mogán**. The vertiginous route winds down along ledges and then a steep scree slope (the remains of a landslide). Fifty minutes downhill, the path bends right across a rocky stream bed. Climbing out of this *barranco*, take the lower path and then turn left downhill alongside the *barranco*. On reaching a track, go right to join a small road, descending to the village of **Las Casillas** and the GC200 (**7h10min**). The BUS STOP lies a minute to the left.

## Walk 21: DEGOLLADA DE LA ALDEA • INAGUA • DEGOLLADA DE LA ALDEA

**Distance/time:** 14.5km/9mi; 5h45min

**Grade:** strenuous, with two tough ascents (300m/1000ft and 450m/1500ft) and overall descents of over 700m/2300ft. You must be sure-footed and have a head for heights. Only suitable in fine weather. Dangerous after wet or windy weather due to rockfall.

**Equipment:** hiking boots, sunhat, long trousers, jacket, fleece, windproof, picnic, *plenty of water*

**Access and return:** 🚌 38 from Puerto de Mogán to/from the Degollada de la Aldea (Timetable 18; journey time 50min). Or by 🚗: park at the viewpoint at the Degollada de la Aldea, south of San Nicolás.

**Short walk:** Degollada de la Aldea — Montaña del Viso — Degollada de la Aldea (8.5km/5.3mi; 2h55min). Moderate, with an ascent/descent of 320m/1050ft. Otherwise grade as above. Equipment and access as above. Follow the main walk up to the 1h15min-point, cross the track, and continue along the ridge to the trig point on Montaña del Viso, less than 20min away. Return the same way.

**Alternative walk:** Circuit of Inagua (12km/7.4mi; 5h15min). Fires in 2007 turned the ascent from the Inagua houses to the Brujas Pass into a barren uphill slog. The pine forest is regenerating very well, but this alternative avoids this section altogether; it is also slightly shorter, with a bit less climbing. Access and grade as main walk (ascents/descents of some 600m/1970ft overall). Follow the main walk to the 1h05min-point, then turn right along the escarpment. If you notice a faint path to the right some 15 minutes along, ignore it. At a clear junction (1h35min), turn left. This mostly-level path takes you to a track (2h10min). Follow this up to the right in zigzags, to the Degollada de las Brujas (2h35min), then pick up the main walk again at the 3h05min-point.

This hike takes you into the nature reserve of Ojeda, Inagua and Pajonales. Buzzards pierce the silence with their shrill cries. Woodpeckers can be heard chipping away on tree trunks, partridges startle you as they fly up from your path, and you may even catch sight of the two large lizards (*lagarto canarión* and *lisa*) found here. Circling Montaña Inagua, you'll be rewarded with stupendous panoramas over the hills of the relatively- inaccessible northwest.

**The walk begins** at the Mirador de Tasártico at the **Degollada de la Aldea**. Ascend the path climbing the hillside just south of the lookout point/parking bay (on your left, as you face in the direction of Mogán). The route circles a massive crown of rock that towers above — **Montaña Inagua**. The view here encompasses the farming settlement of Tasarte lying along an inhospitable *barranco* floor. After five minutes, when you cross to the left-hand side of the ridge, San Nicolás reappears, where a sprawl of greenhouses covers the low valley floor. The summits above are covered in a fringe of pines. An assortment of flora grows out of the sheer rocky walls:

105

salvia, *sonchus, Artemisia,* the cliff thistle, *taginaste, verode,* and *Aeonium.*

Scramble up a rocky strip of hillside. A little further up, at a fork, the path bears left, following a shelf in the incline; ignore the path to the right (**15min**). Soon the cliffs are towering directly overhead, and the colours in the rock begin to catch your attention: grey-green, cream, and mauve — all splashed with marigold-coloured lichen.

Later there is a short stretch of exposed path along a narrow ledge (**40min**). Leaving the ledge, a steady ascent takes you up through scrub and enormous boulders. Some 25 minutes from the ledge, keep left at a fork (**1h05min**). *(But for the Alternative walk, take the path to the right — it is also the return route for the main walk.)* The path now becomes a little hard to follow. Just continue in the same direction, aiming for the crest above, guided by a series of CAIRNS.

Once on the crest, make for a TRACK over to the left (**1h15min**). Over the crest a view unfolds into a basin and the remains of a derelict outpost — the Casas de la Inagua — your next 'landfall'. There is also a superb view inland to enjoy, taking in Roque Nublo and Roque Bentaiga, the Caldera de Tejeda and Artenara. The ravine to the left is the Barranco de la Aldea, which empties out of the Caldera de Tejeda.

Now follow the track to the right. *(But for the Short walk, continue along the top of the ridge to the left.)* Thirty minutes down the track (just after ignoring turnings to both the right and the left), you reach the derelict outpost of **Casas de la Inagua** (**1h45min**), seen earlier. You'll be surprised to find cultivated terracing nearby. Beyond the buildings, ignore a track to the left. Head up into the valley, passing by all turnings to the left.

The track winds its way up through Canary pines to a pass, the **Degollada de las Brujas** (**3h05min**), where there is a junction of tracks, some tables and a spring. You leave the track here, to circle the heights of **Montaña de Ojeda**, which rubs shoulders with Montaña Inagua to the right. Head up the ridge on your right; there is no strongly-discernible path but, 50m/ yds uphill, you will come to a faint path curving left round the hillside. Follow

it; *don't* continue up the ridge. The rest of the nature reserve now comes into view over the treetops — there's a superb rest spot under 10 minutes along, with fine views across the valley. The path is narrow but clear, remaining fairly level as it rounds the steep, dramatic mountainside.

Coming back to the south side of Ojeda, the contour path joins a path ascending from the left (from the Aula de la Naturaleza). The rocky outcrop with the aerial below you at this point is **Roque el Castillete (3h25min)**. Continuing the circuit, follow this new path to the right, across the sheer rock face. This exhilarating route traverses ledges high in the escarpment, with far-reaching views over the inhospitable valleys in the northwest. (These valleys, explored in Walk 22, hide my favourite beach, the Playa de Güigüí.) Below is the village of Tasarte and a valley full of greenhouses. The Degollada de la Aldea creeps back into the picture.

A good half hour past Roque el Castillete the main path bends right (there is a short-cut straight ahead, but it's steep). Some 150m/yds further on, you come to the turn-off right taken in the Alternative walk (**4h05min**). Turn sharp left here on the main path. As the path threads its way through Canary pines, if you become engulfed in mist, remember to remain on the left side of the basin. Re-entering *Cistus* and *tabaiba,* you should see your outgoing track ahead.

In another half hour or so, as you approach a battered

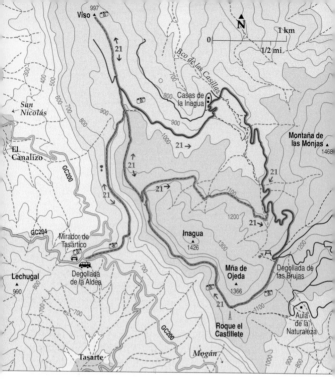

sign, 'RESERVA NATURAL INTEGRAL — INAGUA' (**4h 40min**), you reach your turn-off back down to the Degollada de la Aldea: just a few small CAIRNS alert you to it. The path drops down over the rocky crest. Descend the side of the ridge diagonally to the right, stepping down shelves of rock, to rejoin your outgoing route and turn left.

Some 55 minutes down this path, it is suddenly blocked by stones. Turn right here, to scramble down the rocky hillside encountered at the beginning of the walk, and descend your outgoing route back to the *mirador* at the **Degollada de la Aldea (5h45min)**.

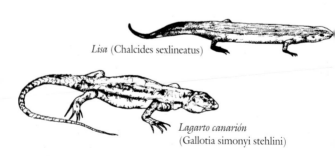

*Lisa* (Chalcides sexlineatus)

*Lagarto canarión*
(Gallotia simonyi stehlini)

# Walk 22: ALBERCON • PLAYA DE GÜIGÜI • TASARTICO

See map page 114

**Distance/time:** 16km/10mi; 7h35min

**Grade:** very strenuous, with an overall ascent of 1350m/4450ft. You must be sure-footed and have a head for heights. The walk is potentially dangerous in wet weather and not recommended in very hot weather.

**Equipment:** walking boots, sunhat, long trousers, long-sleeved shirt, fleece, windproof, rainwear, picnic, *plenty* of water and fruit

**Access:** 🚌 38 from Puerto de Mogán to Albercón (Timetable 18; journey time about 1h10min). A *very early* start is advisable (on 🚌 01 departing Las Palmas at 05.00 and Playa del Inglés/Maspalomas at 06.05; see Timetable 22), so consider spending the night in San Nicolás. (If you *do* spend the night in San Nicolás, you can take an early morning 🚌 115 to Albercón; not in the timetables, but departs San Nicolás at 07.00, 08.00.)
*To return:* 🚖 pre-arranged taxi from Tasártico to San Nicolás or walk (1h30min) from Tasártico to the junction with the main GC200 road at the Degollada de la Aldea, to catch 🚌 38 to Puerto de Mogán (Timetable 18; journey time 40min).

**Shorter walk: Tasártico — Playa de Güigüí — Tasártico** (10km/6mi; 5h40min). Strenuous, with an overall ascent of 900m/3000ft; otherwise grade as above. Equipment as above. 🚖 to/from Tasártico (at the end of the GC204, southwest of the Degollada de la Aldea). From the end of the tarred road in Tasártico, continue downhill on a gravel road for just under 1km. The cairned path to the beach ascends the hillside on the right, between the 5th and 6th power pole below the village. A signpost marks the turning. Follow the path round the hillside, into the narrow Cañada de Aguas Sabinas and cross to the left side. Your immediate goal is the Degollada de Aguas Sabinas, the pass between Montaña de Agua to the left and Montaña de las Vacas to the right — a tough climb, with slippery gravel under foot. From the pass (1h) the path descends in zigzags to the floor of the Barranco de Güigüí Grande. Some 30 minutes down, the path crosses to the right-hand side of the *barranco* and heads to the right of a farmhouse (there may be a sign here, 'Beach'). After crossing the floor of the *barranco* once more, you pass another isolated house. Then you come to some ruins (El Puerto) and, finally, the first beach, Playa de Güigüí Grande. Return the same way.

Spectacular and unique are the only words to describe this walk. Hidden in a cataclysm of harsh, mountainous terrain, Playa de Güigüí is only accessible by sea or on foot. Your path winds up sheer *barranco* walls, briefly hugs the rocky summits, then plunges into the depths. Unexpected greenery floods the valley floors, fed by springs that trickle down through the rocks. Your destination, a sandy beach set at the foot of jagged crags saturated in volcanic mauves and maroons, is for me the most beautiful beach in the entire archipelago.

**Start the walk** in **Albercón**, on the GC200 road, northwest of San Nicolás. There are no signs to indicate that you have arrived at Albercón, but a large building

('ASOCIACION DE VECINOS LA MILAGROSA') with an attached bus shelter stands just before the wide tarred road where the walk begins. Follow this road uphill (to the left, when coming from San Nicolás). It soon reverts to a narrow lane. Keep straight uphill, ignoring tracks both to the right and to the left. After 20 minutes' climbing, you pass a couple of houses on the right. Some three minutes beyond them (about 100m/yds past a large water tank above the track), turn right for Playa de Güigüí on a clearly-defined path (which should be signposted by the time you use this book). But in any case the route is very straight-forward.

Leave civilisation and enter a world of rock carpeted in *aulaga* (a brittle, thorny bush), *verode*, *tabaiba* and great clumps of *cardón* (candelabra spurge). These last are very impressive and can grow to a circumference of 35m/100ft or more (see photograph page 101). Some way along, pass by the remains of a BUILDING (**50min**); ignore the turning left just beyond it. Cross a *barranco*, then climb past a house at the **Degollada de Vallehermoso**. From this pass the path heads left and steeply uphill. In winter, white-flowering *taginaste* covers the slopes. Now you enter a narrow valley, and the ascent becomes even steeper, as you zigzag up the plant-congested *barranco*. Eventually you cross the top of the ridge at the **Degollada del Peñon Bermejo** (**2h05min**), and the San Nicolás valley disappears from view.

Over the crest a spectacular view unfolds — if the wind doesn't knock you off your feet first: razor-sharp ridges sliding down into the deep **Barranquillo del Peñon Bermejo**. Beyond the ridges lies the sea, a thrilling sight and all the more so in early-morning light. The path heads left along the crest and, after a few minutes, the descent begins: take the main path down to the right (ignore the faint path continuing left along the crest). You come into another valley, the **Barranco de Güigüí Chico** (Little

Güigüí). A small farm lies far below. The descent is steep, over loose stones and gravel. Ridges pour down all around, and you'll be amazed at the greenery and colour in this barren landscape. Purple-flowering Canary sage catches your attention, its fern-shaped leaves used to cure throat and gum infections. Another medicinal plant here, *pasote (Chenopodium ambrosioides),* a silvery-grey bush with green berries, is used to alleviate digestive disorders.

After 15 minutes' descent, ignore a minor path to the left. Some 20 minutes later, you pass below a lived-in CAVE DWELLING up to the right (**2h45min**). Then the path swings left, to round a big mound of rock on the hillside. The valley floor is a thicket of green: rushes, cane, *verode, melosilla, tabaiba,* and big bushy palms. A small stream trickles out from the vegetation. A little way upstream, you'll find a spring *(fuente).* Sheer bliss! A yappy dog appears somewhere around here; it belongs to some 'alternative lifestylers', who assure me it's all bark and no bite! Two minutes beyond the stream, you pass a rustic stone and wood cottage which, together with the cave dwelling, are the only habitations in this valley. The path runs alongside this house and then ascends to the left. Occasional bushes of *lingua de gato* (cat's tongue) line the route … it's the bush that keeps sticking to you.

Playa de Güigüí, a small stretch of sand far below, is briefly glimpsed between rocky crags as you ascend the left

111

wall of the valley. Rounding the side of the ridge, some walkers may find a short strip of path unnerving. The final descent to the beach begins when you cross over into the **Barranco de Güigüí Grande** (Big Güigüí; **3h30min**). Abandoned terracing lies along the palm-adorned floor of the valley. Pyramid-shaped hills crown the far ridges. The landscape is austere and desolate, an exhilarating setting for a hike.

The route turns back towards the source of the *barranco*. Massive thick-trunked *tabaiba* bushes flank the path. After 15 minutes downhill, at a fork, keep right and descend through enormous clumps of candelabra spurge. In late spring little red buds adorn each finger of this plant; in flower they are a magnificent sight. Near the valley floor, the way forks, but soon rejoins. Cross the cane-filled STREAM BED (**4h15min**) and, a minute up the far side, come to a small RESERVOIR. Take the path straight ahead (the right-hand fork) and cross terraced plots. Passing to the left of a DERELICT HAMLET, return to the valley floor and cross it again. Several minutes later, recross the valley for a third time. Keep right, round the hillside, again heading towards the bed of the *barranco*. Some minutes later, near a house on the hillside, look out for a path to the left (by a ROCK WITH TWO ARROWS; **4h35min**): this is your return route.

Just beyond this path, cross a tributary, take the first right turn and cross the main stream bed again. Passing below an inhabited house, turn left and step your way down the narrow mouth of the *barranco,* to **Playa de Güigüí Grande (4h45min).**

*Playa de Güigüí*

Unless it's low tide, you'll be confronted with a stony shoreline. The sandy part of the beach (**Playa de Güigüí Chico**) is 10 minutes further along to your right, round a nose of cliff, but only accessible (and, more important, leaveable ...) at low tide. You're surrounded by overwhelming scenery with massive cliffs all around. Brilliant green sea lavender with vivid yellow flowers sprouts out from the rocks. There's piped drinking water here too, beside the stone hut.

If you've set out early enough, you'll have time to bask in these surroundings before tackling the return route. Retrace your steps uphill as far as the small tributary. Then take the well-trodden path that passes to the left of the farm (which has guard dogs). You should spot a colony of beautiful ice plants (once traded for their soda content). The leaves appear to be covered in tiny droplets of ice ... crystal-clear *papillae*.

A *barranco* bed becomes your route a few minutes up from the second house. Keep straight uphill, ignoring paths to the left. Two minutes up, you're back on the left bank of the ravine and, 40 minutes from the beach, you cross the stream bed. Further uphill, telephone wires head in roughly the same direction as your ongoing path. Ignore a minor path to the right. The *camino* winds its way up into the rocky precincts of the summits. Walking with your back to this spectacular view is a sin!

Some 1h40min uphill from the beach, you cross the **Degollada de Aguas Sabinas** (**6h25min**) and bid farewell to the Barranco de Güigüí Grande. Start the descent to Tasártico, down the steep, narrow **Cañada de Aguas Sabinas**. *Attention: the path is gravelly and slippery.* Goats' paths criss-cross the *barranco*, but stay on the right-hand side of the *barranco* for about 40 minutes, until you see telephone lines crossing the valley. Here follow a path cutting across to the left wall of the valley, and continue descending. Rounding the hillside, the **Barranco de Tasártico** opens up. Greenhouses patch the lower walls. On reaching a gravel road (**7h15min**), follow it to the left. After a climb of 20 minutes, your taxi should be waiting in tiny **Tasártico** (**7h35min**). If not, telephone for a taxi from the bar ... yes, a bar, where beer has never tasted better! (If it is closed, rap on the next door.)

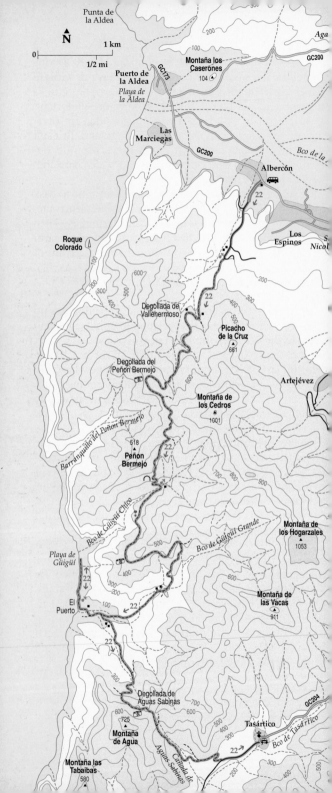

## Walk 23: DEGOLLADA DEL SARGENTO • CRUZ DE MARIA • (ALTAVISTA) • SAN NICOLAS

Map begins on page 121; ends overleaf; *photo: Embalse del Parralillo from Montaña Altavista*

Distance/time: 17km/10.5mi; 5h35min

Grade: fairly strenuous and long, with an overall descent of 1200m/4000ft and ascent of 100m/330ft. You must be sure-footed and have a head for heights. Only suitable in fine weather.

Equipment: walking boots, sunhat, fleece, windproof, raingear, picnic, *plenty of water*

Access: 🚐 18 to Tejeda (Timetable 20) or 🚐 220 to Artenara (Timetable 7), then taxi to the Degollada del Sargento, below Cruz de María.

*To return:* 🚐 38 from San Nicolás to Puerto de Mogán (Timetable 18; journey time 1h), then see Walk 20 on page 102 to continue

by bus to either Playa del Inglés or Las Palmas.

Short walk: Degollada del Sargento — Montaña Altavista — Degollada del Sargento (8.5km/5.3mi; 3h 15min). Fairly easy, with ascents/descents of 300m/1000ft. Otherwise grade, equipment, access as main walk (ask the taxi driver to wait for you or return for you). By 🚐: park at the Degollada del Sargento, on the GC216 road to Tamadaba. Follow the main walk to the 1h20min-point (the turnoff to San Nicolás), then ascend to the left on a shoulder of Montaña Altavista. Ignore the minor path to the left just after turning. Remain on the path until you reach the summit (1h55min). Allow some 1h20min to return the same way.

Although this trek to San Nicolás is a bit long, it crosses spellbinding terrain of immense beauty. If you don't want to tackle the main hike (or you have a car), the short walk to Montaña Altavista is ideal — it takes in the best of the scenery and is a tremendous viewpoint.

**Start the walk** by following the wide *camino real* up the ridge above the *mirador* at the **Degollada del Sargento**. After a few minutes' steep ascent you come to the **Cruz de María**, where you fork left uphill on another path. *(Walk 24 goes right here.)* Climbing through lichen-clad *Cistus* bushes, ignore two minor paths to the right, five minutes apart. Heading southwest along the pine-wooded ridge, you are soon greeted by superb views. To the left lies the deeply-gouged Caldera de Tejeda. The prominent 'standing' rock on the far side of the *caldera* is Roque Nublo; Roque Bentaiga rises in the middle. To the right, the majestic El Teide pierces the white mantle of cloud hovering over Tenerife. And not far below the sharp hills of Tirma drop off into the ocean.

Just after a steep winding descent, and three minutes after passing by a minor path to the left, you come to an

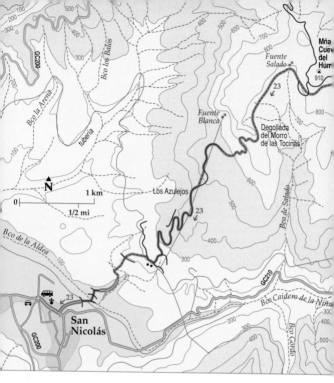

important JUNCTION (**1h20min**; see map above). The main walk goes right here, towards San Nicolás. *(The Short walk climbs left to Altavista. If you are doing the main walk and take this detour, allow an extra 50min.)*

The mountain path is now vertiginous at times. Thirty minutes from the junction, the main path is blocked by stones, so take a brief detour to the right. The sea glistens over to the right, beyond scrub-covered slopes. When you mount the crest of a ridge (**2h**), the glistening greenhouses of San Nicolás come into sight. The path now meanders along the crest. To the left the landscape is bare and barren, but to the right there are signs of reforestation. The lone outpost below to the right is Casas de Tirma, and there's another outpost down in the *barranco* to the left. But the feeling of isolation is overpowering.

The path wanders to either side, but never ventures far from the top of the crest. Approaching Montaña Cueva del Humo, you finally leave the crest and descend its left side. Great gulches slice their way inland, and patches of cream, orange, and pink rock come underfoot. Cross a TRACK (**3h**) descending into the deep valley below. A few minutes later, the path runs alongside the same track, below **Montaña Cueva del Humo**, and then turns left

116

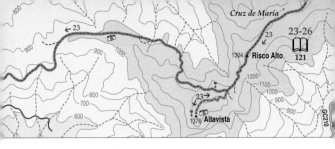

into the **Barranco de Salado**. Five minutes later, still rounding this immense valley, you cross another track. This track is crossed again below a makeshift SHELTER built into the rocky embankment. A few minutes later you cross the *barranco* at **Fuente Salado**.

You leave the valley at the pass of **Degollada del Morro de las Tocinas (3h45min)**, descending towards San Nicolás on a splendid stretch of rose- and maroon-coloured path, overlooking greenhouses covering the valley floor. The stone-paved *camino* leads down onto a lower plateau. Fifteen minutes below the pass, turn right on a minor, unused track.

In the evening, as the hills take on a rosy hue, this descent is quite spectacular. When the track crosses a water pipe, leave it and follow the water pipe to the left (a short-cut). The patch of bluish rock in the hillside below is **Los Azulejos**. Rejoining the track, continue downhill. Below the plain, do *not* follow another track which runs parallel with your route for a short stretch (as it later bends back to the right). The main route is rough and stony. Ignore a track to the left and, three minutes later, come to some ABANDONED BUILDINGS (**4h55min**). Turn right at the T-junction here. After two minutes, beyond the buildings, descend a wide old *camino* to the left (marked by a cairn). Five minutes downhill, the path bends left to meet a minor track at a T-junction. Turn left and, after 10m/yds, turn right to rejoin the path (*take care* on this rough descent).

Reaching the FLOOR OF THE VALLEY (**5h15min**), turn left on another path. After a couple of minutes, some houses signal civilisation. At the fork that follows, keep right; then turn left at a T-junction. Pass through an intersection and then go right at the next T-junction. Just over a *barranco* bed, asphalt comes underfoot. Entering **San Nicolás**, turn right at a T-junction. Keep straight on through a pedestrian walkway, then along a street, until you reach the *plaza* and CHURCH (**5h35min**). The BUS STOPS (bus 101 and bus 38) are some 100m/yds south of the roundabout, on the town side of the road (there is a stop on the park side, but it is only used for dropping off).

## Walk 24: ARTENARA • TAMADABA • LAS PRESAS • SAN PEDRO

More photos pages 1, 11, 50

**Distance/time:** 17.5km/11mi; 5h10min

**Grade:** moderate-strenuous, but the 1000m/3300ft descent to San Pedro is very steep and often gravelly (dangerous in bad weather); you must be sure-footed and have a head for heights.

**Equipment:** walking boots, sunhat, long trousers, long-sleeved shirt, warm fleece, windproof, raingear, picnic, water

**Access:** 🚌 220 to Artenara (Timetable 7) or 🚌 18 to Tejeda (Timetable 20), then 🚕 taxi (928 666161) to Artenara
*To return:* 🚌 102 from San Pedro to Gáldar (Timetable 1; departs a few minutes after leaving Los Berrazales; journey time 40min), then any of frequent 🚌 to Las Palmas (and on to Maspalomas/Playa del Inglés)

🚗 **Motorists:** See page 122 for circular walk suggestions.

**Short walk: Tamadaba — Las Presas — San Pedro** (6.2km/3.8mi; 2h25min). Grade and equipment as main walk. Access: 🚕 taxi from Artenara to the picnic area at Tamadaba. Return as main walk. Pick up the main walk at the 2h45min-point, at the turn-off for the *zona recreativa* (picnic area), and follow it to the end.

Tamadaba boasts the best pine forest on Gran Canaria. While getting there involves a good stretch of hiking along the road, outside Sundays and holidays there's little traffic, and the views from the road are splendid. Green slopes roll off the *cumbre* down into gullies holding little reservoirs. Lichen-draped pine trees forest the summits. Las Presas (the reservoirs) is an enchanting woodland setting of mirror-still reservoirs ensconced amidst pine trees. A steep and dramatic descent drops you down into the lush floor of Agaete Valley. Halfway down, hidden in a hillside, lies a fascinating ancient Guanche site.

**Start out** at the BUS STOP in the centre of **Artenara** below the church square. Walk down the road descending past the park. A few minutes down, at a roundabout, go straight across, climbing the road to the 'CEMENTERIO'. Just beyond the CEMETERY and HELICOPTER PAD, the road forks (**15min**): keep left uphill, first on tarmac and then along a track. Continue straight ahead along the wooded crest *(Walk 26 turns off left)*, with excellent views across the parched, sharply-lined Caldera de Tejeda. To the right lie the rolling pastures of the northwest.

Circling to the right of **Montaña Brezos**, the track ends. Bear left on a path (paved at first). Descend through pines and scrub and, when you meet the Tamadaba road (GC210), turn left. Go straight through an intersection and, five minutes later, turn left to rejoin your ascending path (**1h**). When you meet a road again (the GC216), turn left. After 150m/yds, you come to a *mirador* at the **Degol-**

*Looking down over Agaete, from the viewpoint 3h35min into the walk*

**lada del Sargento**. It overlooks the raised flat-topped lava tongue of the Vega de Acusa, shown on page 4 (Walk 26).

Ascend the steps to the right of the *mirador* and, after a couple of minutes, come to the **Cruz de María** (**1h 20min**), where the path forks. *(Walk 23 takes the left fork here.)* Keep right, and ignore the next two turnings to the left. Descending to the road again, turn left and pass the pretty **Casa de Tirma**, a forestry house. Some 100m/yds further on, turn left to rejoin your path. Then meet the road yet again and follow it straight ahead.

After 15 minutes on the road, you enter the forest again (**2h15min**). At the first deep bend to the left, just past a small *barranco* crossed by a low stone wall, look carefully for your path to the right. Descend into the *Cistus*. After three minutes, ignore a path down to the right; keep on a level contour. Some five minutes later, a brief 'all-fours' scramble over rocks leads you back up to the road. Cross it, and climb the embankment opposite, to pick up a continuing minor path. After three minutes, a path joins from the left. Continue over the crest and pass through an intersection. Tall slender pines, with long wispy beards of lichen, make this a magical stretch. *Cistus* layers the floor, at times blocking the way, and asphodels flourish.

Back on the road, continue downhill to the left. After about eight minutes, turn right to the **Zona Recreativa/ Zona Acampada de Tamadaba** (**2h45min**; Picnic 24, photograph page 11). A few minutes downhill, where the road curves to the left, keep straight ahead on a track, past the coach park (ZONA APARCAMIENTO DE GUAGUAS). Follow a rough track through a picnic area, ignoring a turning to the left. Skirt a vehicle barrier and, 250m/yds further on, turn left (sign: CAMINO DE SAN PEDRO') on a walled-in *camino real* which rounds a private farm (**Casas de Tamadaba**). *Important: you are on private land, which walkers have permission to cross, but please keep to the main trail and observe any 'no swimming' notices.* Keep an eye open for delicate, pink-flowering *Micromeria pineolens,* a species endemic only to the Tamadaba forest.

Further on various tracks and paths cross the route; *always continue on the walled-in* camino. You pass to the left of a picturesque RESERVOIR (the first of several), set amidst pines (**3h10min**); on the left there's a splendid avenue of cypress trees. Further downhill, another reservoir appears to the right. Soon, rounding the hillside, spectacular views open up through the trees, down onto sharp desiccated valleys and out over the sea. Several minutes later, just beyond a water channel, the view fans from the Barranco de Agaete below round to the prominent Pico de Gáldar on the right. You can keep straight ahead here by following the path to the left for a couple of minutes, to a fine viewpoint at a high jutting crag — but don't go too near the edge!

Back on the main route (**3h35min**), turn left: your magnificent path now winds down the sheer side of the ridge with a succession of more splendid views. Grazing goats bleat out across the valley walls. Lower down the path passes through a landscape littered with boulders.

Some 40 minutes from the viewpoint at the crag, you descend to a cream and brown-coloured volcanic cone piercing the hillside (**Roque Bermejo**; **4h15min**), by a restored wheat-threshing floor. The *camino* circles to the right of the cone, *down a very slippery, steep path.* Five minutes later, you're looking up at an ancient aboriginal colony consisting of some 50 caves carved into a volcanic tube — the **Cuevas de Berbique**. Entrances — circular, square, and arched — cover the deep red- and wine-coloured face of the escarpment, a breathtaking sight!

Reaching a V in the *barranco* wall, the *camino* bends sharply down to the left (a little way to the right, you'll find a spring), and crosses the *barranco* a minute later. Now head along a hillside above almond trees and cross a tributary. San Pedro slowly reveals itself. Coming down the nose of a crest, ignore a path to the right and reach an INTERSECTION (**4h55min**). *Don't* go sharp right here: take the lower path, following the street lamps. Almost immediately, turn back to the left, keeping down the nose of the ridge. Two paths join you from the left. When you reach a driveway, follow it to the village road. Turn right and, after a few minutes, reach the CHURCH and plaza in **San Pedro** (**5h10min**). Climb the steps opposite the church, to the main road. The BUS STOP lies 100m/yds along the road to the right.

## Walk 25: ARTENARA • EL HORNILLO • LOS BERRAZALES OR SAN PEDRO

See map page 121; see also photographs pages 1, 50

**Distance:** 11.5km/7mi; 3h25min to Los Berrazales; 12.5km/7.8mi; 4h to San Pedro

**Grade:** easy descent of 1000m/3300ft. Not suitable in bad weather. One very short stretch of vertiginous path near the end of the walk.

**Equipment:** walking boots, sunhat, fleece, jacket, long trousers, rain-gear, picnic, water

**Access:** 🚌 220 to Artenara (Timetable 7) or 🚌 18 to Tejeda (Timetable 20), then 🚖 taxi (928 666161) to Artenara
*To return:* 🚌 102 from the Hotel Princesa Guayarmina in Los Berrazales or from San Pedro to Gáldar (Timetable 1; journey time 40min; bus departs San Pedro a few minutes after Los Berrazales), then any of frequent 🚌 to Las Palmas (and on to Maspalomas/Playa del Inglés)

🚗 **Motorists:** Waymarked trails between Tamadaba and the reservoirs of Lugarejos and Los Pérez (see purple lines on the map) allow you to plan two wonderful circuits linking Walks 24 and 25, but both involve strenuous ascents. For the northerly circuit from Los Berrazales allow a good 7-8h (ascent/descent of 1000m/3300ft; for a southerly circuit from Artenara about 7h (ascent/ descent of 700m/2300ft). Use the map to follow the walks in reverse where necessary.

It's easy, it's all downhill, and it's packed with mouth-watering scenery. This hike crosses grassy hills to dip into low-slung valleys which cradle fairly large reservoirs. White-faced cave dwellings adorn the valley walls, while the magnificently-sited village of El Hornillo, with houses built into the side of the cliff, is the showpiece of the walk.

**Start out** at the BUS STOP in the centre of **Artenara**, below the church square. Walk downhill on the road descending past the park. When you come to a roundabout, take the GC210 towards San Nicolás, passing above the FOOTBALL PITCH. Some 300m/yds further on, turn right down a concrete lane, into the **Barranco de la Coruña**. The village of cave dwellings opposite is **Las Cuevas**. Keep straight down the crest, ignoring turnings to the right. Near the bottom of the *barranco,* the lane reverts to track. When you reach a TELEPHONE POLE ON THE LEFT WITH THE NUMBER 26, turn left down a path (**30min**).

Descending, you pass a row of apple trees. Terracing with citrus trees and vegetable plots steps the hillside below. Almost immediately you're on a narrow path going off into grass, down into the *barranco.* In winter the pleasant sound of trickling water will keep you company. After a few minutes on the path, by a VIADUCT crossing a tributary, descend steps to the right and cross the stream. The path then runs alongside a covered watercourse. Ignore a path to the left.

Several minutes later, by two tiny RESERVOIRS in the

valley floor, cross the RESERVOIR WALL and continue on the path (overgown with grass in winter) as it goes left round the top of the crest, passing below a WATER TANK. Edging a garden plot, you come to a STONE HUT after a couple of minutes. Turn left, walk below the hut, and make for the road. Follow the road uphill to the right. After 10 minutes you pass a row of four adjoining houses on the right (**55min**). Just past the last house, climb a cobbled path, cross a tarred road, and go straight ahead on a track, past a ELECTRICITY TRANSFORMER STATION on the right.

The track runs across a gentle grassy slope. When the track ends, continue to the right over a slight embankment, from where a cobbled path takes you round the side of the crest. Descending into the **Barranco de Lugarejos**, you spot the Embalse de Lugarejos over to the left. Five minutes from the track, the path runs alongside a stream in the *barranco* bed. Head left along the stream and, two minutes later, cross it on a small FOOTBRIDGE. In spring the banks here are aglow with bright purple *Senecio*. A few minutes later you join a concrete lane, which leads you onto another lane. Continue straight ahead through **Lugarejos** (**1h20min**), a strung-out village overlooking the reservoir. After five minutes, the lane ends. Continue on a path running off it and, at a fork, keep right. Continue uphill and cross the low ridge where the last of the villages houses are clustered. Go through an intersection, bearing right. Now you are greeted by an impressive view over a khaki-coloured reservoir. Large aloes hem in the path.

After five minutes' walking along the side of a slope, at a fork, turn left downhill to the road below. Turn right and circle the reservoir, the **Embalse de los Pérez**, passing a friendly BAR/SHOP (**1h55min**). A minute later, a superb view greets you — the Barranco de Agaete, dropping away into a dark corridor of rock.

To reach El Hornillo, the next stop, continue up the steep road from the reservoir. Five minutes uphill, turn left at a junction. On rounding a bend, El Hornillo dramatically appears. This green little foothold can be seen opposite, nestling high on a shelf in the valley walls. The white-washed *casitas* seem to be squeezed into gaps in the sheer face of the cliff rising above the village, and steeply-terraced plots teeter on the brink. Bright yellow *sonchus* spots the walls. When you reach the CHURCH SQUARE in **El Hornillo** (**2h15min**), take a break to admire the view into the upper realms of the **Barranco de Agaete**.

Cross the balcony viewpoint and go down the steps.

*Embalse de los Pérez*

Turn left at the bottom and, a couple of minutes later, keep right at a fork. This path takes you downhill past the remains of an old FLOUR MILL (the original millstone is still beside it). Following a worn cobbled path, pass through the colourful hillside hamlet of **El Sao** and descend to the ROAD (**2h50min**). Five minutes down the road, turn left on an old *camino* (marked by YELLOW DOTS).

Crossing a pass, you look straight down onto the HOTEL PRINCESA GUAYARMINA and surrounding orchards. A steep descent follows (take care on the slippery pine needles). *If you are ending the walk at Los Berrazales,* look out for a goats' path on your right (**3h20min**). You can finish off the walk in style by sliding down this path on your bottom, to the road in **Los Berrazales**. Then walk the few minutes to the BUS STOP, just above the hotel.

*To make for San Pedro,* instead of sliding down the goats' path, keep straight ahead (there is a vertiginous stretch of path just above the road). Pass by a bridge, and head straight down the cobbled path. Soon you enter a *barranco* bed, which leads you down to a track. Follow the track to the right, up to the road, and turn left. After two minutes on the road, just past a TELEPHONE KIOSK, turn left onto another path. Citrus and advocado groves line the valley floor. Some minutes along, cross a lane and walk along the right-hand side of a football pitch. Pass a building and keep straight ahead, skirting a STONE WALL on your right. A paved path then takes you onto the village road. Turn right for the plaza and CHURCH in **San Pedro** (**4h**) Opposite the church, ascend a flight of steps up to the main GC231. The BUS STOP lies 100m/yds along the road to the right.

# Walk 26: ARTENARA • VEGA DE ACUSA • ARTENARA

See map page 121; see also photographs pages 1, 4, 50

**Distance/time:** 15km/9.3mi; 5h30min

**Grade:** fairly strenuous; the return is all uphill. Ascents/descents of about 700m/2300ft. You must be sure-footed and have a head for heights. Not recommended in bad weather.

**Equipment:** walking boots, sunhat, long trousers, long-sleeved shirt, warm fleece, windproof, raingear, picnic, *plenty of water*

**Access and return:** 🚌 220 to/from Artenara (Timetable 7; convenient return bus on *Sundays and holidays only*) or 🚌 18 to/from Tejeda (Timetable 20), then 🚖 taxi (928 666161) to/from Artenara. Or 🚗: park in Artenara (or in Acusa, to avoid a climb at the end of the walk).

**Shorter walk:** Artenara — Acusa Seca — Artenara (9.5km/6mi; 3h 50min). Moderate-strenuous, with a descent/reascent of 500m/1650ft. Not recommended in wet weather. Equipment, access/return as main walk. Follow the main walk as far as Acusa Seca (1h40min), then return.

T he Vega de Acusa is an elevated plain lodged in the great Barranco de Tejeda. This immense tongue of lava juts out into the valley, almost completely severed by *barrancos*. It's a tableland of greens and dusty yellows, immersed in a landscape of sharp ridges. Ensconced in the valley walls lies the rejuvenated little village of Acusa Seca, hewn out of the cliffs falling off the *vega*. And just below this hamlet are some long-abandoned cave dwellings, with white-bordered doorways opening out of the sheer towering valley walls — an intriguing sight.

**Start out** at the BUS STOP in the centre of **Artenara** below the church square. Walk downhill on the road descending past the park. A few minutes down, at a roundabout, go straight across, climbing the road to the 'CEMENTERIO'. Just beyond the CEMETERY and HELI-COPTER PAD, the road forks (**15min**): keep left uphill, first on tarmac and then along a track. Coming to a small parking area (from where there is a superb view of the sharp and severe ridges in the Barranco de Tejeda), take the path to the left, running just below your ascent track. This path takes you into the upper confines of the Barranco de Tejeda.

Shortly the Vega de Acusa comes into full view. It's the most prominent feature in the landscape — a raised plateau of cultivation, poured out into a stark upheaval of ridges. Acusa itself, no more than a church, an abandoned school and a couple of houses, is clearly visible on this tableland. The hillsides are patchily wooded, and white-flowering *Cistus*, *tabaiba*, and *retama* grow out of the rocky terrain. The noticeable rock off to the right of the tableland is Montaña Altavista, visited in Short walk 23.

Cross a TRACK (**50min**). The path, faint at times, heads

down a rocky ridge with small CAIRNS for guidance. Keep to the left-hand side of the crest. When you come to a low WALL (**1h15min**), turn left alongside it, making your way around some plots. On reaching a road, turn left and follow it for five minutes, to a CROSS by a narrow road on the left signposted 'ACUSA SECA'. This is where you begin your circuit round the **Vega de Acusa**. Take this road; soon you descend into the **Barranco de Tejeda**. Cane and abandoned plots fill the valley floor. The largest of the rock crags on the opposite ridge is Roque Bentaiga, with Roque Nublo (Walk 1) in the background (photograph page 4). The large settlement set back in the left of the *barranco* is Tejeda.

At the end of the road you enter the hamlet **Acusa Seca** (**1h40min**). *(The Shorter walk turns back here.)* Now you leave the road: take the wide path that descends round the slope, passing some small RENOVATED HOUSES bordered by colourful gardens. After a few minutes, on rounding a bend, the amazing sight shown opposite stops you in your tracks! Small doorways, neatly bordered in white, open out from the sheltered rock face, bringing to mind an ancient sanctuary. The path continues downhill past this curious sight (Picnic 26). CAVES and doorways appear all along the way. The lower ones are particularly intriguing.

Five minutes downhill, keep right at two forks in quick succession. Before rounding the hillside, take one last look back up at the village. The path now hugs the hillside at the foot of cliffs. At first it's clear, but it soon narrows into a rough and vertiginous animals' trail. Half an hour from Acusa Verde, you arrive at a small GUANCHE SETTLEMENT (**2h10min**), caves set in the sheer cliffs above. Half a minute later, a protruding rock makes an excellent lookout spot. A tiny, partially-concealed settlement lies below to the right, resting on the edge of a cultivated flat area. And beyond it, the Barranco de Tejeda narrows into a twisting corridor of jagged rock. A slippery descent follows, through a colony of strident-green, soft-needled *valo*. Keep to the foot of the cliffs, passing caves all the way along. On joining a farm track, follow it out to the ARTENARA/SAN NICOLAS road (GC210) and turn right. Almost immediately, you pass through **Acusa Verde** (**2h 45min**). (There's a water tap on the right just before the first house, or you can stop at the BAR EL CHORROS.)

From here you will follow the (little-trafficked) road for well over an hour. Before long, you pass some immaculate little houses squeezed under the roadside cliffs, almost hidden by their exuberant, overflowing gardens. You pass the ACUSA JUNCTION (**3h30min**), where a half-empty reservoir lies below and then the CROSS at the ACUSA SECA JUNCTION (**3h45min**). Leave the road about five minutes later: head right, to ascend to Artenara by your outgoing path. The path is a little more difficult to find in this direction, until you cross the track, after which the way becomes quite straightforward. Back at the junction below the SCHOOL in **Artenara**, turn right. A few minutes later, you'll see a cobbled path climbing up left into the village centre (**5h30min**).

*The cave houses below Acusa Seca (Picnic 26)*

# BUS TIMETABLES

*Below is a list of destinations covered by the following pages of timetables. Numbe*
*following place names are* **timetable numbers.**

## Buses for the north and the interior

### 1 Bus 102 Gáldar to El Valle (Los Berrazales); *daily*

| Gáldar | Agaete° | Los Berrazales• |
|--------|---------|-----------------|
| 10.30 | 10.55 | 11.10 |
| 14.30 | 14.55 | 15.10 |
| 16.30 | 16.55 | 17.10 |

°Bus reaches Puerto de las Nieves 5min later; •Bus reaches San Pedro a few minutes before L
Berrazales

| Los Berrazales• | Agaete° | Gáldar |
|-----------------|---------|--------|
| 07.40 | 07.55 | 08.20 |
| 11.40 | 11.55 | 12.20 |
| 15.40 | 15.55 | 16.20 |
| 19.40 | 19.55 | 20.20 |

•Passes San Pedro a few minutes after Los Berrazales; °Reaches Puerto de las Nieves 5min later

### 2 Bus 103 Las Palmas to Puerto de las Nieves; *daily*

| Las Palmas | Gáldar | Pto. de las Nieves* | Pto. de las Nieves° | Gáldar | Las Palmas |
|------------|--------|---------------------|---------------------|--------|------------|
| 07.00 | 07.45 | 08.15 | 06.30 | 07.00 | 07.45 |
| and every hour on the hour until | | | and every hour on the half hour• until | | |
| 22.00 | 22.45 | 23.15 | 23.30 | 23.00 | 00.45 |

*Bus reaches Agaete 5min earlier; °Bus reaches Agaete 5min later; •at 09.00, 10.00, 13.00, 14.0
17.00, 18.00 buses also leave on the hour (two buses an hour to Las Palmas)

### 3 Bus 105 Las Palmas to Gáldar; *daily*

| Las Palmas | San Andrés | Gáldar | Gáldar | San Andrés | Las Palmas |
|------------|------------|--------|--------|------------|------------|
| 06.30 | 06.55 | 07.15 | 06.30 | 06.50 | 07.15 |
| and every hour on the half hour until | | | and every hour on the half hour until | | |
| 23.30 | 23.55 | 00.15 | 23.30 | 23.50 | 00.15 |

### 4 Bus 101 Gáldar to San Nicolás; *daily*

| Gáldar | Agaete *Mon-Sat* | San Nicolás | San Nicolás | Agaete *Mon-Sat* | Gáldar |
|--------|-------|-------------|-------------|-------|--------|
| 07.30 | 07.50 | 09.10 | 07.30 | 08.50 | 09.10 |
| 07.45* | 08.05 | 09.25 | 09.00 | 10.20 | 11.40 |
| 11.15 | 11.35 | 12.55 | 14.00 | 15.20 | 15.40 |
| 15.45 | 16.05 | 17.25 | 17.30 | 18.50 | 19.10 |
| 19.30 | 19.50 | 21.10 | | | |
| *Sundays/holidays* | | | *Sundays/holidays* | | |
| 07.30 | 07.50 | 09.10 | 09.00 | 10.20 | 11.40 |
| 15.45 | 16.05 | 17.25 | 17.30 | 18.50 | 19.10 |

*Not on Sat

## Bus 210 Las Palmas to Arucas; *daily*

| Las Palmas | Arucas | | | Arucas | Las Palmas |
|---|---|---|---|---|---|
| *Mon-Fri* | | | | *Mon-Fri* | |
| 07.10 | 08.05 | | | 06.10 | 06.45 |
| and every 30min until | | | | and every 30min until | |
| 20.40 | 21.15 | | | 20.10 | 20.45 |
| 21.30 | 22.05 | | | | |
| *Sat/Sun/holidays* | | | | *Sat/Sun/holidays* | |
| 08.40 | 09.15 | | | 07.40 | 08.15 |
| and every hour until | | | | and every hour until | |
| 20.40 | 21.15 | | | 19.40 | 20.15 |
| 21.30 | 22.05 | | | 20.30 | 21.05 |
| 22.15 | 22.50 | | | 21.30 | 22.05 |

## Bus 123 Arucas to Moya

| Arucas | Bco. Azuaje | Moya | Arucas | Bco. Azuaje | Moya |
|---|---|---|---|---|---|
| *Mon-Fri* | | | *Sat, Sun and holidays* | | |
| 08.00 | 08.20 | 08.30 | 09.45 | 10.05 | 10.15 |
| 09.50 | 10.10 | 10.20 | 10.15 | 10.35 | 10.45 |
| 11.15 | 11.35 | 11.45 | | | |
| 14.30 | 14.50 | 15.00 | | | |
| 16.00 | 16.20 | 16.30 | | | |

## Bus 220 Las Palmas to Artenara

| Las Palmas | Teror* | Lanzarote | Pinos de Galdár | Artenara |
|---|---|---|---|---|
| | | *Mon-Sat* | | |
| — | 11.00 | 11.30 | 12.05 | 12.20 |
| — | 14.15 | 14.45 | 15.20 | 15.35 |
| 16.15+ | 16.55+ | 17.25+ | 18.00+ | 18.15+ |
| — | 19.00+ | 19.30+ | 20.05+ | 20.20+ |
| | | *Sundays and holidays* | | |
| 08.15 | 08.55 | 09.25 | 10.00 | 10.15 |
| 16.15 | 16.55 | 17.25 | 18.00 | 18.15 |

| Artenara | Pinos de Galdár | Lanzarote | Teror* | Las Palmas |
|---|---|---|---|---|
| | | *Mon-Sat* | | |
| 06.20 | 06.35 | 07.10 | 07.40 | — |
| 12.40 | 12.55 | 13.30 | 14.00 | — |
| 18.45+ | 19.00+ | 19.35+ | 20.05+ | 20.45+ |
| 20.15• | 20.30• | 21.05• | 21.35• | — |
| | | *Sundays and holidays* | | |
| 10.45 | 11.00 | 11.35 | 12.05 | 12.45 |
| 18.45 | 19.00 | 19.35 | 20.05 | 20.45 |

Saturdays only; •Mon-Fri only; *Bus stops at Teror for 15min

## Bus 216 Las Palmas to Teror; *daily*

| Las Palmas | Teror | | Teror | Las Palmas |
|---|---|---|---|---|
| 06.30 | 07.15 | | 06.00 | 07.45 |
| 07.30 | 08.15 | | and every hour on the hour* until | |
| 08.00 | 08.45 | | 20.00 | 20.45 |
| and every hour on the hour until | | | | |
| 21.00 | 21.45 | | | |

But no bus at 08.00 Mon-Fri

## 9 Bus 303 Las Palmas to San Mateo; *daily*+

| Las Palmas | Tafira Alta | Santa Brigida | San Mateo |
|---|---|---|---|
| 06.00 | 06.20 | 06.35 | 06.50 |
| | and every half hour until | | |
| 22.30 | 22.50 | 23.05 | 23.20 |

+stops outside the Botanical Garden in Tafira Alta

| San Mateo | Santa Brigida | Tafira Alta | Las Palmas |
|---|---|---|---|
| 05.30 | 05.45 | 06.00 | 06.20 |
| | and every half hour until | | |
| 22.00 | 22.15 | 22.30 | 22.50 |
| 23.30 | 23.45 | 00.00 | 00.20 |

## 10 Bus 305 Las Palmas to Tejeda; *daily**

| | San Mateo | Las Lagunetas | Cruz de Tejeda | La Culata | Tejeda |
|---|---|---|---|---|---|
| | 19.00 | 19.20 | 19.35 | 20.00 | 20.20 |
| | 20.00 | 20.20 | 20.35 | — | 21.20 |

| Tejeda | La Culata | Cruz de Tejeda | Las Lagunetas | San Mateo | Las Palmas |
|---|---|---|---|---|---|
| 06.10+ | 06.40+ | 07.05+ | 07.20+ | 07.40+ | 08.30+ |
| 06.30• | 07.00• | 07.25• | 07.40• | 08.00• | — |
| 13.00 | — | 13.55 | 14.10 | 14.30 | — |
| 15.00 | — | 15.55 | 16.10 | 16.30 | — |

*Important note:* For morning departures, first take 🚌 303 (Timetable 9, above) to San Mateo and change to 🚌 18 (Timetable 20); +Mon-Fri only; •Sat only

## 11 Bus 311 Las Palmas to Bandama*; *daily*

| Las Palmas | Tafira Baja | Bandama | Bandama | Tafira Baja | Las Palmas |
|---|---|---|---|---|---|
| 05.55 | 06.15 | 06.40 | 06.50 | 07.05 | 07.25 |
| and every hour at 55min | | | and every hour at 40min | | |
| past the hour until | | | past the hour until | | |
| 20.55 | 21.15 | 21.40 | 21.40 | 22.05 | 22.25 |

*This bus passes through La Atalaya 10min before reaching Bandama and passes through La Atalaya 10min after departing from Bandama

# Buses for the south

## 12 Bus 12 Las Palmas to Telde; *daily*

| Las Palmas | Telde | | Telde | Las Palmas |
|---|---|---|---|---|
| 06.00 | 06.25 | | 06.25 | 06.50 |
| and every half hour until | | | and every half hour until | |
| 21.30 | 21.55 | | 22.25 | 22.50 |

## 13 Bus 13 Telde to Tenteniguada; *daily*+

| Telde | Valse–quillo | Tenteni-guada | Tenteni-guada | Valse-quillo | Telde |
|---|---|---|---|---|---|
| 07.45• | 08.00• | 08.10• | 08.35• | 08.45• | 09.00• |
| 08.45 | 09.00 | 09.10 | 09.35 | 09.45 | 10.00 |
| 09.45• | 10.00• | 10.10• | 10.35• | 10.45• | 11.00• |
| 10.45 | 11.00 | 11.10 | 11.35 | 11.45 | 12.00 |
| 11.45• | 12.00• | 12.10• | 12.35• | 12.45• | 13.00• |
| 13.45• | 14.00• | 14.10• | 14.35• | 14.45• | 15.00• |
| 14.45 | 15.00 | 15.10 | 15.35 | 15.45 | 16.00 |
| 15.45 | 16.00 | 16.10 | 16.35 | 16.45 | 17.00 |
| 16.45 | 17.00 | 17.10 | 17.35 | 17.45 | 18.00 |
| 17.45• | 18.00• | 18.10• | 18.35• | 18.45• | 19.00• |
| 19.45 | 20.00 | 20.10 | 20.45 | 20.55 | 21.10 |
| 21.35 | 21.40 | 21.50 | 22.15 | 22.25 | 22.50 |

+'San Mateo' bus; •Sundays only

## 4  Bus 11 Las Palmas to Agüimes*; *daily*

| Las Palmas | Carrizal | Agüimes | Agüimes | Carrizal | Las Palmas |
|---|---|---|---|---|---|
| 06.50 | 07.20 | 07.35 | 06.00 | 06.15 | 06.45 |
| and every hour until | | | and every hour until | | |
| 21.50 | 22.20 | 22.35 | 22.00 | 22.15 | 22.45 |

There are a few extra buses at busy times. **Bus 21** also runs to Agüimes *Mon-Fri only;* departs Las Palmas at 20min past the hour from 07.20 to 19.20; departs Agüimes at 30min past the hour from 6.30 to 16.30 (but no bus at 14.30)

## 5  Bus 34 El Doctoral to San Bartolomé; *daily*

| El Doctoral | Agüimes | Santa Lucía | San Bartolomé |
|---|---|---|---|
| 07.30* | 07.45 | — | — |
| 08.00 | 08.15 | 08.45 | 09.05 |
| 11.00* | 11.15* | 11.45* | 12.05* |
| 12.00 | 12.15 | 12.45 | 13.05 |
| 13.25* | 13.40* | — | — |
| 14.00* | 14.15* | 14.45* | 15.05* |
| 16.30 | 16.45 | 17.15 | 17.35 |
| 19.30 | 19.45 | 20.15 | 20.35 |

Not on Sat, Sun or holidays

| San Bartolomé | Santa Lucía | Agüimes | El Doctoral |
|---|---|---|---|
| 06.45 | 07.05 | 07.35 | 07.50 |
| 08.00* | 08.20* | 08.50* | 09.05* |
| 09.30* | 09.50* | 10.20* | 10.35* |
| 10.00+ | 10.20+ | 10.50+ | 11.05+ |
| 12.30* | 12.50* | 13.20* | 13.35* |
| 14.30 | 14.50 | 15.20 | 15.35 |
| 18.00 | 18.20 | 18.50 | 19.05 |

Not on Sat, Sun or holidays; +Sat, Sun and holidays only

## 6  Bus 60 Las Palmas to Aeropuerto; *daily*

| Las Palmas | Aeropuerto | Aeropuerto | Las Palmas |
|---|---|---|---|
| 00.30 | 01.00 | 00.00 | 00.30 |
| 01.30 | 02.00 | 01.00 | 01.30 |
| 05.45 | 06.15 | 02.00 | 02.30 |
| 06.00 | 06.30 | 06.15 | 06.45 |
| 06.45 | 07.15 | 06.50 | 07.20 |
| then every hour on the hour | | then every hour at 15min | |
| and at 45min past the hour until | | and 50min past the hour until | |
| 20.00 | 20.30 | 20.50 | 21.20 |
| 21.30 | 22.00 | 22.00 | 22.30 |
| 22.30 | 23.00 | 23.00 | 23.30 |
| 23.30 | 00.00 | | |

## 7  Bus 66 Faro de Maspalomas to Aeropuerto; *daily*

| Faro de Maspalomas | Aeropuerto | Aeropuerto | Faro de Maspalomas |
|---|---|---|---|
| 06.15 | 07.30 | 07.20 | 08.35 |
| then every hour until | | then every hour until | |
| 20.15 | 22.30 | 22.20 | 23.35 |

## 18  Bus 38 Puerto de Mogán to San Nicolás; *daily*

| Puerto de Mogán | Mogán | Deg. de la Aldea | San Nicolás |
|---|---|---|---|
| 06.45* | 06.55* | 07.25* | 07.45* |
| 07.00 | 07.10 | 07.40 | 08.00 |
| 11.30• | 11.40• | 12.10• | 12.30• |
| 16.00 | 16.10 | 16.40 | 17.00 |
| 19.30• | 19.40• | 20.10• | 20.30• |

| San Nicolás | Deg. de la Aldea | Mogán | Puerto de Mogán |
|---|---|---|---|
| 08.00 * | 08.20* | 08.50* | 09.00* |
| 09.00 | 09.20 | 09.50 | 10.00 |
| 14.05• | 14.25• | 14.55• | 15.05• |
| 17.30 | 17.50 | 18.20 | 18.30 |

*Mon-Fri only; •Not Sundays or holidays. The bus stops at Las Casillas a few minutes before/after Mogán.

## 19  Bus 30 Las Palmas to Playa del Inglés* and the Faro de Maspalomas (via the motorway)

| Las Palmas | Maspalomas |
|---|---|
| *Mon-Fri* | |
| 06.30 | 07.55 |
| and then thrice-hourly at 05min, 25min, 45min past the hour until | |
| 19.55 | 21.20 |
| 20.35 | 22.00 |
| 21.05 | 22.30 |
| *Sat, Sun and holidays* | |
| 06.30 | 07.55 |
| and then twice-hourly at 30min and 50 min past the hour until | |
| 20.50 | 22.15 |

| Maspalomas | Las Palmas |
|---|---|
| *Mon-Fri* | |
| 07.15 | 08.40 |
| and then thrice-hourly at 10min 30min, 50min past the hour until | |
| 20.50 | 22.15 |
| 21.25 | 22.50 |
| *Sat, Sun and holidays* | |
| 06.00 | 07.25 |
| and then twice-hourly on the hour and half-hour until | |
| 20.30 | 21.55 |
| 21.25 | 22.50 |

*Goes through the centre of Playa del Inglés; terminus at the Faro de Maspalomas. ***Important:*** most buses leave Las Palmas from the Santa Catalina station, *not* San Telmo; *recheck!*

## 20  Bus 18 Faro de Maspalomas — San Bartolomé — Cruz Grande — Ayacata — Tejeda — San Mateo; *daily**

| Faro de Maspalomas | San Bartolomé | Cruz Grande | Ayacata | Tejeda | San Mateo |
|---|---|---|---|---|---|
| 08.00 | 08.50 | 09.40 | 09.50 | 10.00 | 11.00 |
| 11.00 | 11.50 | 12.40 | 12.50 | 13.00 | — |
| 15.00 | 15.50 | 16.40 | 16.50 | 17.00 | 18.00 |
| 17.00 | 17.50 | 18.40 | 18.50 | 19.00 | 20.00 |
| 19.00 | 20.00 | — | — | — | — |

| San Mateo | Tejeda | Ayacata | Cruz Grande | San Bartolomé | Faro de Maspalomas |
|---|---|---|---|---|---|
| 08.00 | 09.00 | 09.10 | 09.20 | 10.10 | 11.00 |
| 11.00 | 12.00 | 12.10 | 12.20 | 13.10 | 14.00 |
| 14.15 | 15.15 | 15.25 | 15.35 | 16.25 | 17.15 |
| 16.00+ | 17.00+ | 17.10+ | 17.20+ | 18.10+ | 19.00+ |

***Important:*** This bus normally goes *into* the village of La Culata, but check with the driver beforehand
+All times one hour later on Sundays/holidays

## 1 Bus 45 Bahía Felíz to Los Palmitos; *daily*

| Bahía Felíz | Playa del Inglés | Los Palmitos | Los Palmitos | Playa del Inglés | Bahía Felíz |
|---|---|---|---|---|---|
| 09.30 | 09.40 | 10.00 | 13.30 | 13.50 | 14.00 |
| 10.00 | 10.10 | 10.30 | 14.00 | 14.20 | 14.30 |
| 10.30 | 10.40 | 11.00 | 14.30 | 14.50 | 15.00 |
| 11.00 | 11.10 | 11.30 | 15.00 | 15.20 | 15.30 |
| 11.30 | 11.40 | 12.00 | 15.30 | 15.50 | 16.00 |
| 12.00 | 12.10 | 12.30 | 16.30 | 16.50 | 17.00 |
|  |  |  | 17.30 | 17.50 | 18.00 |
|  |  |  | 18.00 | 18.20 | 18.30 |

## 2 Bus 01 Las Palmas to Puerto de Mogán

| Las Palmas | Puerto Rico | Puerto de Mogán | Puerto de Mogán | Puerto Rico | Las Palmas |
|---|---|---|---|---|---|
|  | *Mon-Fri* |  |  | *Mon-Fri* |  |
| 05.00 | 06.25 | 06.45 | 07.10 | 07.30 | 08.55 |
| and every 20min until |  |  | and every 20min until |  |  |
| 19.20 | 20.45 | 21.05 | 19.50 | 20.10 | 21.35 |
| 20.30 | 21.55 | 22.15 |  |  |  |
| 21.30 | 22.55 | 23.15 |  |  |  |
| 22.30 | 23.55 | 01.15 |  |  |  |
| 23.30 | 01.55 | 02.12 |  |  |  |
| *Sat, Sun and holidays* |  |  | *Sat, Sun and holidays* |  |  |
| 05.00 | 06.25 | 06.45 | 07.00 | 07.20 | 07.45 |
| and every 30min until |  |  | and every 30min until |  |  |
| 19.30 | 20.55 | 21.15 | 19.30 | 19.50 | 21.15 |

## 3 Bus 32 Playa del Inglés to Puerto Mogán; *Mon-Sat*

*Mon-Fri*

| Playa del Inglés | Arguineguín | Puerto Rico | Puerto Mogán |
|---|---|---|---|
| 08.35 | 08.50 | 09.00 | 09.25 |
| then every half-hour at 05min and 35min past the hour until |  |  |  |
| 19.05 | 19.20 | 19.30 | 19.55 |
| 20.05 | 20.20 | 20.30 | 20.55 |

| Puerto Mogán | Puerto Rico | Arguineguín | Playa del Inglés |
|---|---|---|---|
| 07.55 | 08.10 | 08.20 | 08.45 |
| 08.55 | 09.10 | 09.20 | 09.45 |
| 09.55 | 10.10 | 10.20 | 10.45 |
| then every half-hour at 25min and 55min past the hour until |  |  |  |
| 18.25 | 18.40 | 18.50 | 19.15 |
| 19.25 | 19.40 | 19.50 | 20.15 |

*Saturdays*

| Playa del Inglés | Arguineguín | Puerto Rico | Puerto Mogán |
|---|---|---|---|
| 09.05 | 09.20 | 09.30 | 09.55 |
| then every half-hour at 05min and 35min past the hour until |  |  |  |
| 13.35 | 13.50 | 14.00 | 14.25 |

| Puerto Mogán | Puerto Rico | Arguineguín | Playa del Inglés |
|---|---|---|---|
| 08.55 | 09.10 | 09.20 | 09.45 |
| 09.55 | 10.10 | 10.20 | 10.45 |
| then every half-hour at 25min and 55min past the hour until |  |  |  |
| 13.25 | 13.40 | 13.50 | 14.15 |
| 14.25 | 14.40 | 14.50 | 15.15 |

## 24 Bus 84 Puerto Mogán to Mogán; *daily*

| Puerto Mogán | Mogán | | Mogán | Puerto Mogán |
|---|---|---|---|---|
| 08.00 | 08.15 | | 08.30 | 08.45 |
| and every hour on the hour until | | | and every hour on the half-hour until | |
| 12.00 | 12.15 | | 12.30 | 12.45 |
| then | | | then | |
| 16.30 | 16.45 | | 17.00 | 17.15 |
| 17.30 | 17.45 | | 18.00 | 18.15 |
| 18.30+ | 18.45+ | | 19.30+ | 19.45+ |
| 19.30• | 19.45• | | 20.00• | 20.15• |
| 21.40 | 21.55 | | 22.00 | 22.15 |

+Not Sundays or holidays; •Only Sundays/holidays

# ● *Index*

Geographical names comprise the only entries in this index. For other entries, see Contents, page
4. A number in **bold type** refers to a photograph; a number in *italic type* refers to a map. Both
may be in addition to a text reference on the same page. *TM* refers to the walking map on the
reverse of the pull-out touring map. Pronunciation is indicated for some place names, in case you
have to ask the way or instruct a taxi driver.